1954

WHAT A YEAR TO BE BORN!

Written by
Robin Bennett-Freebairn and Joe Toussaint

Published by Emersive
www.whatayeartobeborn.com

What happened in 1954? Most of us have a special affinity for the year we were born, but how much do we really know about it? This guide takes you through the highs and lows of an historic year in the midst of the baby boom generation. The colour-coded chapters unlock a wealth of information, bringing you closer to what life was like in this special year.

Contents

▶ Introduction

First and foremost there is one thing to get out of the way when discussing 1954. The 11th April that year has been defined by computer analyst William Tunstall-Pedoe as the most boring day in history after he trawled 300 million facts on the internet. Too bad if you were born on that day or voted in the Belgian general election, which took place then. Thankfully, for both reader and writer much else happened during the year. In Britain, the last remnants of wartime rationing were lifted so it was steaks all round as restrictions on the sale of meat ended. It is not known how many steaks Roger Bannister had for his supper before running at Iffley Road track in Oxford on 6th May, but he broke the four-minute mile barrier for the first time. A year after Edmund Hillary and Tensing Norgay conquered Mount Everest, an Italian expedition successfully ascended K2, the second highest peak, albeit not before a fight near the top. Popular boys' names for the year were David, John and Stephen. For girls it was Susan, Linda and Christine. The population of the UK was around 51 million with London around 8 million. Though few noticed it at the time, a young man named Elvis Presley released his first single *That's All Right*, but it failed to chart. The world of television saw two debuts featuring animals. In America, *Lassie* the ultimate rescue animal made her debut. In the UK, David Attenborough first presented *Zoo Quest* where he and his team scoured the globe for animals to bring back to British zoos. Floods in China saw an estimated 33,000 lose their lives in the Yangtze Delta, whilst in Austria an avalanche in Blons killed hundreds and displaced thousands.

The art world saw the deaths of two of its greatest exponents, losing both Henri Matisse and Frida Kahlo. In cinema, a highly acclaimed adaptation of George Orwell's *Animal Farm* was released. Hitchcock was at his mysterious best directing both *Dial M For Murder* and *Rear Window*. In Japan, Akira Kurosawa directed *The Seven Samurai*, a film which has spawned many imitations. The world of science also lost two of its greatest minds. Alan Turing, who saved millions of lives through his genius of code breaking, was hounded to his death because of his sexuality. Enrico Fermi, who escaped Fascism to first help create 'The Bomb' and then campaign against it, died in November. He was the architect of the Fermi Paradox which is a contradiction between the high probability of extraterrestrial life and the lack of evidence for it. This brings us nicely on to Ann Hodges of Alabama who was asleep when a meteorite crashed through her roof, ricocheted and injured her. She thought it would bring her great fame and fortune, but it didn't and ended up as a doorstop.

We hope as you delve into this book it will rekindle childhood memories. Toys you may have played with, music your parents may have listened to and films you were taken to the cinema to see. We also hope that we bring you one or two surprising facts about the remarkable year you were born.

The Daily Headlines

No: 5136

Price: Three pence

Evening Edition

Thursday, January 14, 1954

MARILYN MONROE AND BASEBALL PLAYER JOE DIMAGGIO MARRY AT SAN FRANCISCO CITY HALL

The Daily Headlines

Price: Three pence

Thursday, January 21, 1954

No: 5143

Evening Edition

THE WORLD'S FIRST NUCLEAR POWERED SUBMARINE IS LAUNCHED IN THE UNITED STATES

The Daily Headlines

Price: Three pence

Thursday, May 6, 1954

No: 5259

Evening Edition

ROGER BANNISTER SHATTERS THE FOUR MINUTE MILE BARRIER IN NEW WORLD RECORD

The Daily Headlines

No: 5300

Price: Three pence

Evening Edition

Tuesday, June 8, 1954

SECOND WORLD WAR CODE BREAKER ALAN TURING IS FOUND DEAD AT HIS HOME IN SUSPECTED SUICIDE BY CYANIDE POISONING

Jan 1ˢᵗ   The Soviet Union (Russia) ceases to demand World War II reparations from West Germany.

Jan 3ʳᵈ   In the US, the last steam driven passenger locomotive leaves Washington Union Station bound for Richmond, Virginia.

Jan 6ᵗʰ   A light aircraft carrying a rugby team crashes near Albury in Hertfordshire. All bar one on board perish.

Jan 10ᵗʰ   BOAC Flight 781, a de Havilland Comet jet plane, disintegrates in mid-air due to metal fatigue and crashes in the Mediterranean near Elba. All 35 people on board lose their lives.

Jan 11ᵗʰ   George Cowling presents the first in-vision weather forecast in the UK. He shares meteorological duties with Tom Clifton. They would soon become known as Mr. Shower and Mr. Shine.

Jan 12ᵗʰ   A crowd of over 50,000 gather to watch Queen Elizabeth II attend the State Opening of Parliament in Wellington, New Zealand.

Jan 12ᵗʰ   Avalanches in the Austrian Alps leave more than 200 dead.

Jan 14ᵗʰ   So here's to you Joe DiMaggio. The most famous baseball player of his generation, 'The Yankee Clipper', marries Hollywood icon Marilyn Monroe in the wedding of the year.

Jan 18ᵗʰ   British character actor and "man you would like to have a beer with" Sydney Greenstreet dies. He appeared in *Casablanca*, *The Maltese Falcon* (for which he received an Oscar nomination) and *They Died With Their Boots On*.

Jan 21ˢᵗ   The world's first nuclear-powered submarine, the USS Nautilus, is launched in Groton, Connecticut. First Lady Mary Geneva 'Maime' Eisenhower performs the ceremony.

Jan 25ᵗʰ   Dylan Thomas's Under Milk Wood is broadcast for the first time on BBC radio with an all-Welsh cast led by Richard Burton and Rachel Thomas.

Feb 2nd — President Dwight D. Eisenhower reveals that the United States successfully detonated a Hydrogen Bomb in 1952.

Feb 3rd — Queen Elizabeth II becomes the first reigning British monarch to visit Australia. She is welcomed by the Governor General Viscount Slim.

Feb 3rd — It's Chinese New Year. Those born before February 3rd are in the year of the Water Snake being both calm and able to overcome adversity. Those born after fall within the year of the Horse and are clever, active and popular.

Feb 10th — After authorising $385 million above the $400 million already budgeted for military aid to Vietnam, President Eisenhower warns against his country's intervention in the region.

Feb 19th — The Soviet Union officially cedes Crimea to Ukraine, which is part of the USSR.

Feb 28th — Children in America show that it is right to bare arms as the first mass vaccination of youngsters against polio takes place in Pittsburgh Pa.

Mar 1st — Puerto Rican nationalists launch an attack on the chamber of the House of Representatives in Washington DC. Five politicians are injured. The perpetrators are immediately arrested.

Mar 3rd — 'Leave room for a brown derby'. American chain Wimpy opens its first bar in Lyons Corner House in Coventry Street, London.

Mar 12th — Germany and Finland formally declare an end to their state of war.

Mar 13th — Milan High School (with only 161 attendees) defeats Muncie Central High (enrolment over 1,600) to win the Indiana State basketball title.

Mar 19th — At Madison Square Garden in New York, the first colour televised boxing match sees Joey Giardello knock out Willie Tory.

Mar 21st — Fire breaks out at a school in Cleveland Hill, USA. The building is made entirely of wood. 15 sixth grade students are killed. A law is passed prohibiting wooden buildings from housing schools.

Mar 25th   The 26th Academy Awards are held simultaneously in Hollywood and New York. They are televised live for the second time and draw an audience of over 43 million. *From Here to Eternity* scoops best picture and its director Fred Zinneman also takes the top award. William Holden is Best Actor for his role in *Stalag 17* and Audrey Hepburn is Best Actress for her part in *Roman Holiday*.

Mar 25th   The Radio Corporation of America produces its first colour television set. It retails for $1,000, one quarter of an average person's yearly wage. Unfortunately most shows are still recorded in black and white.

Mar 28th   The British troop ship the HMT Windrush suffers an engine room fire. Four crew members are killed, but 1494 crew and passengers are saved. The abandoned ship later sinks.

Mar 30th   The United Nations Department of Economic and Social Affairs (Population Division) gives the population of the world as 2,691,979,339. China is the most populous country with 589,936,004 people, India is second with 389,731,406 and The United States is third with 158,205,873. The United Kingdom is in ninth position with 50,969,939. How can they be so precise?

Apr 2nd   Plans are announced by Walt Disney for a theme park in Anaheim California. The provisional name is Disneylandia. One wonders if they will come up with a catchier name!

Apr 3rd   The 100th Boat Race takes place on the River Thames. The dark blues of Oxford University run out winners against Cambridge University.

Apr 6th   The Flags and Emblems (Display) Act (Northern Ireland) comes into force. It makes it illegal to interfere with the Union Flag or display a flag likely to cause a breach of the peace.

Apr 14th   Creator of the National Health Service Aneurin 'Nye' Bevan resigns from the Shadow Cabinet in protest at the Labour Party's failure to oppose the rearmament of West Germany.

Apr 20th	Murderer Michael Manning becomes the last person to be executed in Ireland.
Apr 22nd	*Secret Love* from the film *Calamity Jane,* sung by Doris Day, takes the No.1 spot in the UK charts and becomes the best-selling record of the year.
Apr 22nd	Senator McCarthy commences hearings investigating the US Army for being 'soft' on communism.
Apr 24th	Wolverhampton Wanderers win the First Division title for the first time. In doing so they deny their local rivals West Brom a chance of 'the Double'.
May 1st	An 87th minute goal by Frank Griffin wins the F.A. Cup for West Bromwich Albion as they run out 3-2 winners against Tom Finney's Preston North End.
May 5th	The American Viking 11 rocket reaches a record height of 158mi (254km), taking the highest altitude photographs of the Earth to date.
May 6th	On a blustery day at the Iffley Road track in Oxford, Roger Bannister breaks the four-minute mile barrier. He breaks the tape in a time of 3:59.4.
May 10th	St. George's Hospital Cardiology Department opens providing groundbreaking cardiac care to the residents of South London.
May 14th	Virginia Margaret Schau wins the Pulitzer prize for photography. She is the first woman and only the second amateur to scoop the prize. Her most iconic photograph *Rescue on Pit River Bridge* was taken using a Kodak Brownie camera.
May 29th	Just 23 days after Roger Bannister broke the four-minute mile, Diane Leather breaks the five-minute mile at the Alexander Sports Ground in Birmingham, becoming the first woman to ever do so.
Jun 3rd	A Soviet MiG-15 fighter jet attacks a Belgian cargo plane killing one person on board. It was travelling between Britain and Yugoslavia, forcing it to land in Austria.

Jun 6th   Pope Pius XII delivers a message via the Eurovision Network, which has been set up by Britain, France, Belgium, The Netherlands, Italy and Switzerland.

Jun 7th   Mathematical genius Alan Turing is found dead by his housekeeper. He is aged just 41.

Jun 7th   Formula 1 racing comes to Cornwall. The compact circuit at Davidstow hosts the fastest cars on the planet. British driver John Riseley-Prichard takes the chequered flag driving a Connaught Type-A.

Jun 12th   An Irish Republican Army unit carries out a successful arms raid on Gough Barracks in Armagh, Northern Ireland. It signals a renewal of Republican paramilitary activity following a long hiatus.

Jun 26th   Fray Bentos pies are off the menu as Uruguay knock England out of the Soccer World Cup. Goals by Nat Lofthouse and Tom Finney are not enough as the South Americans run out 4-2 victors.

Jun 26th   The world's first civilian nuclear power station, the Obninsk Nuclear Power Plant, is commissioned in the Soviet Union.

Jun 29th   Hobson's Choice, directed by David Lean and starring Charles Laughton wins the Golden Bear Award at the 4th Berlin Film Festival.

Jul 2nd   A ballot of Welsh local authorities, carried out by the South Wales Daily News, reveals a preference for Cardiff as the official capital of Wales. Wales has had no capital city since Ludlow in 1689.

Jul 3rd   Czech born, but holder of an Egyptian passport, Jaroslav Drobný becomes the first African citizen to win the Wimbledon Men's Singles tennis championships when he beats Ken Rosewall in the final.

Jul 4th   The 'Mighty Magyars' led by Ferenc Puskás are humbled by the amateurs of West Germany in the Soccer World Cup Final. The Germans win 3-2 in front of a crowd of 62,500 at the Wankdorf Stadium in Bern, Switzerland.

Jul 4th	In the UK, fourteen years of rationing finally come to an end when meat officially comes off the ration list.
Jul 5th	A young man by the name of Elvis Aaron Presley records his first single, *That's All Right,* at Sun Studios in Memphis, USA.
Jul 9th	Australia's Peter Thompson bags himself £750 as he wins the Open Golf Championship at Royal Birkdale. Peter Alliss finishes four shots off the lead.
Jul 15th	Donald McGill, creator of saucy seaside postcards, is found to be too saucy. He is found guilty of breaching the Obscene Publications Act (1857) at a court in Lincoln.
Jul 29th	J.R.R. Tolkien's fantasy novel *The Fellowship of the Rings* is published.
Jul 31st	An Italian led team make it to the summit of the world's second highest peak, K2, but not without much shenanigans on the way up.
Aug 4th	The English Electric Lightning P1 supersonic fighter plane makes its maiden flight. It is capable of travelling at twice the speed of sound.
Aug 4th	The Independent Television Authority begins operations, paving the way for an end to the BBC's monopoly.
Aug 6th	The German airline Luftag buys the name and emblem of the defunct airline Deutsche Luft Hansa. Renamed, Lufthansa, it will start flying in April 1955.
Aug 7th	The Air Force School of Aviation at Randolph Field, Texas takes receipt of the first specially built space cabin simulator.
Aug 16th	The first issue of Sports Illustrated magazine is published. The cover photo, by Mark Kauffman, famously features future third baseman Eddie Mathews at the plate for the Braves at Milwaukee's County Stadium.
Aug 25th	US Air Captain Joseph McConnell dies when the controls of an F-86H Sabre fighter bomber malfunctions at Edwards Air Base in California. Aged just 32, He was the top-scoring American fighter jet ace in history.

Aug 26th   Hurricane Carol leaves a trail of destruction behind in the Bahamas and heads for North Carolina, before taking aim at New York and the New England States.

Sep 3rd   The National Trust of Scotland acquires Fair Isle for the nation to enjoy. It is home to around 30 migratory bird species.

Sep 3rd   After 2,956 episodes spanning a 21-year period, the final 'new' episode of *The Lone Ranger* radio program is broadcast in the USA.

Sep 5th   Kidbrooke School in the London Borough of Greenwich opens as the first purpose built comprehensive school in the UK.

Sep 7th   Smithdon High School in Hunstanton, Norfolk opens its doors to a new intake of secondary school pupils. Designed by Peter and Alison Smithson, it is viewed as a shining example of modernist architecture in a style coined 'New Brutalism'.

Sep 9th   The 1954 series of banknotes is issued in Canada. They feature the recently crowned Queen Elizabeth II as Head of State.

Sep 9th   Long distance swimmer Marilyn Bell becomes the first person to swim across Lake Ontario.

Sep 11th   Roy Race 'Roy of the Rovers' makes his debut for Melchester Rovers and appears on the cover of the *Tiger Comic*. Has he already bought a trophy cabinet?

Sep 11th   Never Say Die completes the Derby/ St. Leger double. He is ridden by jockey Charlie Smirke who has every reason to smile as he stands in for the suspended Lester Piggott.

Sep 14th   Benjamin Britten's opera *The Turn of the Screw* premieres at the Teatro La Fenice in Venice, Italy.

Sep 17th   Rocco Francis Marchegiano aka Rocky Marciano retains his World Heavyweight crown with an eighth round knockout of Ezzard Charles in New York.

Sep 18th *The Last Night of the Proms* features Edward Elgar's 1902 setting of *Land of Hope and Glory*, Hubert Parry's 1916 setting of William Blake's *Jerusalem* and Malcolm Sargent's arrangement of *Rule Britannia*.

Sep 23rd A group of schoolboys armed with knives and sharpened sticks make for Glasgow's Southern Necropolis where a giant vampire was allegedly seen. The authorities blame a fervent imagination and the reading of American comics for the mass hysteria.

Sep 27th Steve Allen presents the first episode of *The Tonight Show* on NBC in America.

Oct 13th Chris Chattaway shatters the world 5000m record, beating the previous mark set earlier in the year by Russian Vladimir Kuts by five seconds.

Oct 14th Having already been awarded the Order of the Elephant by Denmark, The Order of the Seraphim by Sweden and the Order of Merit of the Austrian Republic, Emperor Haile Selassie of Ethiopia arrives in London on a state visit, but leaves empty handed.

Oct 15th Hurricane Hazel slams into Toronto leaving 81 people dead, having already killed around 500 in Haiti.

Oct 18th The MP for Bromley, Harold MacMillan is promoted to the Cabinet for the first time when Prime Minister Winston Churchill makes him Minister of Defence.

Oct 19th A public inquiry into two recent crashes of the de Havilland Comet aircraft hears that metal fatigue was the most likely cause of the disasters which left 50 people dead.

Oct 21st During a visit to Lancashire, Queen Elizabeth II formally opens the John McCurdy Hall of the Wigan Mining and Technical College. The building, which is designed to house up to 3,000 staff and students, cost around £200,000 to complete.

Oct 25th In Salerno, Italy, severe rains produce landslides that claim over 300 lives.

Oct 27ʰ   The movie *Godzilla* debuts in Japan. Director Ishirō Honda filmed Godzilla's Tokyo rampage to mirror the atomic bombings of Hiroshima and Nagasaki and stated: "If *Godzilla* had been a dinosaur or some other animal, he would have been killed by just one cannonball. But if he were equal to an atomic bomb, we wouldn't know what to do. So, I took the characteristics of an atomic bomb and applied them to *Godzilla*."

Oct 28ʰ   It is announced that American author Ernest Hemingway is to be awarded the Nobel Prize in Literature.

Nov 1ˢᵗ   Algerian Nationalists issue The Declaration of 1ˢᵗ November 1954, marking the start of the Algerian Revolution.

Nov 2ⁿᵈ   Although he hasn't yet moved into 23 Railway Cuttings, East Cheam, Tony Hancock brings much mirth to our living rooms with the radio show Hancock's Half Hour. He is joined by Sid James, Hattie Jacques, Bill Kerr and Kenneth Williams.

Nov 8ʰ   Eighteen-year-old local lad Bob Charles beats a top international field to win the New Zealand Golf Open.

Nov 11ʰ   Based on a US Congress amendment passed on 1ˢᵗ June 1954, this is the first observance of Veterans Day, replacing Armistice Day in the United States.

Nov 12ʰ   The newly launched tanker, Scottish Hawk, runs aground in the Clyde in Greenock, Renfrewshire, Scotland.

Nov 13ʰ   Bruce Seton first stars as *Fabian of the Yard*. It is a groundbreaking TV show following police procedure, much like the earlier US series *Dragnet*.

Nov 13ʰ   It's "Allez Grande-Bretagne". The Great Britain team lift the inaugural Rugby League World Cup in a final against France, in front of a packed house at Parc des Princes in Paris.

Nov 27ʰ   Violent storms hit the British Isles leading to two maritime tragedies. The South Goodwin lightship is wrecked with the loss of seven lives, while the tanker World Concord breaks in two in the Irish Sea.

Nov 30th — Winston Churchill becomes the first Prime Minister to celebrate his 80th birthday whilst in office. William Gladstone was the oldest PM, but was not in office when he first became an octogenarian.

Dec 1st — The Hyatt House Hotel, the first hotel attached to an airport, opens in Los Angeles, USA.

Dec 4th — The first branch of Burger King opens in Miami, Florida, USA.

Dec 25th — A BOAC Boeing 377 Stratocruiser crashes on landing at Glasgow's Prestwick Airport killing 28 people.

Dec 25th — Queen Elizabeth II's Christmas message is broadcast to the nation and the Commonwealth. In it she states:

"It is now two years since my husband and I spent Christmas with our children. And as we do so today we look back upon a Christmas spent last year in Auckland in hot sunshine, thirteen thousand miles away. Though this was strange for us, we felt at home there, for we were among people who are my own people and whose affectionate greeting I shall remember all my life long. They surrounded us with kindness and friendship, as did all my people throughout the mighty sweep of our world-encircling journey. Nevertheless, to all of us there is nothing quite like the family gathering in familiar surroundings, centred on the children whose Festival this truly is, in the traditional atmosphere of love and happiness that springs from the enjoyment of simple well-tried things. When it is night and wind and rain beat upon the window, the family is most conscious of the warmth and peacefulness that surround the pleasant fireside. So, our Commonwealth hearth becomes more precious than ever before by the contrast between its homely security and the storm which sometimes seems to be brewing outside, in the darkness of uncertainty and doubt that envelopes the whole world."

Dec 31st — The aptly named Sprinkling Tarn in Cumberland breaks the record for the most rainfall in the UK in one calendar year. Nearly 257 ins (6527mm) fall on the body of water located 3 miles from the village of Seathwaite.

Oprah Gail Winfrey
born on 29th January 1954 in Kosciusko, Mississippi, USA

Oprah is an American talk show host, television producer, actress, author and philanthropist. She is best known for her talk show, *The Oprah Winfrey Show*, broadcast from Chicago. It was the highest-rated television programme of its kind in history running from 1986 to 2011. Dubbed the 'Queen of All Media', she was the richest African-American of the 20th century and was once the world's only black billionaire. By 2007, she was sometimes ranked as the most influential woman in the world. Raised in abject poverty, she received her first pair of shoes at age 6. She learned to read at age 2½, literature has always been important to her. The Book Club section of her show was estimated to have boosted sales by 30 million. Her occasional forays into acting have brought much success. She was nominated for an Oscar for her role in Steven Spielberg's adaptation of Alice Walker's *The Color Purple* (1985). In 1998, she again showcased African-American literature when she starred in and produced a version of Toni Morrison's *Beloved*. Her multi-media company Harpo Productions employs over 10,000 people. Oprah got the name for her company by reversing her own name. Harpo was also the character name of her husband in *The Color Purple*.

The power of Winfrey's opinions and endorsement to influence public opinion, especially consumer purchasing choices, has been dubbed 'the Oprah Effect'. The effect has been documented or alleged in domains as diverse as book sales, beef markets and voting.

Iain Banks
born on 16th February 1954 in Dunfermline, Fife, Scotland

His first published novel, *The Wasp Factory*, which told the story of a multiple killer who lived with his father, appeared in 1984 when Banks was 30 years old. It had been rejected by six publishers before being accepted by Macmillan. It was met with a mixture of critical acclaim and controversy and was described by a critic in the Irish Times as a "work of unparalleled depravity". It did, however, establish Banks as an original voice in Scottish fiction. His first science fiction book, *Consider Phlebas*, was published in 1987 using his assumed middle initial Iain M. Banks. Banks' subsequent novels explored gothic settings, contemporary politics, pop culture and technology. When in April 2013 it was announced that Banks was terminally ill, he met adversity with stoic humour. Stating that he was "officially very poorly", he asked his long-term partner Adele to do him the honour of "becoming my widow". He died on 9th June 2013. The son of Fife left a lasting impact on both science and literary fiction. By the time of his death, he had 26 published novels in print, the 27th *The Quarry* was published posthumously. His novels were notoriously difficult to adapt for silver screen. However, the best efforts were the television productions of *The Crow Road* (1996) and *Stonemouth* (2015).

When Iain's parents registered his birth they had intended to name him Iain Menzies Banks, but his father missed out his middle name.

Michael Anthony Holding
born on 16th February 1954 in Kingston, Jamaica

Michael Holding is one of the greatest fast bowlers to have graced the game of cricket. The youngest of four children, he overcame childhood asthma to become a superb athlete in his teens with a career as a 400m runner beckoning. His family lived near the Sabina Park cricket ground where his interest in cricket was first kindled. From the first time he picked up a cricket ball it was clear that he was a natural born fast bowler. In 1975. he came to the attention of the West Indies Cricket Board and was chosen to be part of the team that toured Australia. The tour was a failure and Holding considered giving up the game. However, the tour of England in 1976 changed everything. One match in particular elevated Holding to the status of greatness. It was at the Oval on a flat pitch where he took 14 wickets while his fellow pace men toiled. Further success followed when they beat Australia on their home patch. After a twelve year test career, he combined erudite cricket commentary with horse breeding through his friendship with a Bajan racehorse trainer. Umpire Harold 'Dicky' Bird christened Holding 'Whispering Death' as his run-up was so smooth that he couldn't hear him coming. Geoffrey Boycott stated that Holding was the fastest bowler that he ever faced, but also thought that he was bowling within himself stating that he was "scary".

Unlike most of his contemporaries Holding has never accepted any honours, save for an honorary degree from the University of East London.

John Joseph Travolta
born on 18th February 1954 in Englewood, New Jersey, USA

Everybody who's ever seen *Saturday Night Fever* remembers Travolta's Tony Manero strutting his stuff to *Stayin' Alive*. It is one of the most iconic moments in movie history. Like his character, Travolta was announcing the arrival of somebody who was confident in his looks and his ability. It is no surprise that Travolta grew up in a showbiz family. His mother Helen was an actress and dancer and enrolled John in drama school. At the age of 18, he landed a role in a Broadway production of the hit musical *Grease*. After that he decided to try his luck in Hollywood and landed parts in *The Rookies* and *Emergency!*. When he auditioned for *Saturday Night Fever* in 1977, director John Badham recognised that Travolta was born for the role. When a year later the role of Danny Zuko in the film *Grease* came up, John was a shoe-in as it was a part he knew off by heart. A golden period followed as he starred in the hugely successful *Urban Cowboy* (1980) and the comedy *Look Who's Talking* (1989) to name but two. Closing this period in Travolta's career was another iconic dance scene when he performed an oh-so-sexy routine with Uma Thurman in *Pulp Fiction* (1994). One to forget is *Battlefield Earth* (2000) where he combined his acting skills with his belief in Scientology in an adaptation of L. Ron Hubbard's book. Away from acting Travolta is also a singer-songwriter having released nine albums. Four of his singles have charted in the Top 40 of the Billboard Hot 100.

"I don't think I'm very cool as a person. I'm just better than anyone else at acting cool."

Sir Anish Mikhail Kapoor CBE, RA
born on 12th March 1954 in Bombay (now Mumbai), India

Famous for his use of abstract biomorphic forms and his penchant for rich colours and polished surfaces, Kapoor was the first living artist to be given a solo show at the Royal Academy of Arts in London. Born to a Hindu Father and a Jewish mother, Kapoor had a Jewish upbringing. After a time on a Kibbutz in Israel, he studied electrical engineering. He then moved to England to attend Hornsey College of Art (1973-77) and Chelsea School of Art and Design (1977-78). During a visit to India he immersed himself in the art of the land of his birth and started on his early sculptures, which were characterised by simple curved forms. With this methodology, Kapoor produced bodies of work such as *1000 Names* which became part of his first high-profile exhibit in the New Sculpture exhibition at the Hayward Gallery London in 1978. He produced a number of large works, including *Tarantara* (1999), *Parabolic Waters* (2000) and *Marsyas* (2002), a monumental structure commissioned for Tate Modern's Turbine Hall. His most famous (some would say infamous) structure was the 376ft high *Orbit Tower 2011* created for the 2012 London Olympics. He was knighted in 2013 and received an honorary doctorate degree from the University of Oxford in 2014. In 2017, he set up the Anish Kapoor foundation as a charity to further public appreciation of art.

Richard Morrison of *The Times* described *Orbit* as "like an enormous wire-mesh fence that has got hopelessly snagged round the bell of a giant french horn", adding that it "seems like an awful lot of trouble just to look at East London."

Jackie Chan
born on 7th April 1954 in British Hong Kong

When his parents moved from Hong Kong to Australia to find new jobs, the 7-year-old Chan was left behind to study at the Chinese Opera Research Institute, a Hong Kong boarding school. For the next 10 years, he studied martial arts, drama, acrobatics and singing, and was subjected to stringent discipline, including corporal punishment for poor performance. He appeared in his first film, the Cantonese feature *Big and Little Wong Tin Bar* (1962), when he was only eight. He then went on to appear in a number of musical films. Once considered a likely successor to Bruce Lee in Hong Kong cinema, Chan instead developed his own style of martial arts blended with screwball physical comedy. He became a huge star throughout Asia and went on to have hits in the United States as well as in China. He produced impressive action comedies such as *Project A* (1983), *Police Story* (1985) and *Armor of God* (1986), as well as the hit period film *Mr. Canton and Lady Rose* (1989), a clever remake of Frank Capra's 1961 film *A Pocketful of Miracles*. Hits in Hollywood included the *Rush Hour* franchise alongside Chris Tucker and *The Forbidden Kingdom* (2007). In 2010 he starred with Jaden Smith in a remake of the 1984 film *The Karate Kid*. In 2011, *1911* was Chan's 100th movie. In 2016, he was the second highest paid actor in the world. He was also listed in Forbes magazine's list of the top 10 most charitable celebrities.

Chan never took his craft too seriously, stating that his true heroes were Buster Keaton and Harold Lloyd.

 Trevor John Francis
born on 19th April 1954 in Plymouth, UK

Trevor Francis was one of the golden boys of English football during the 1970s and 80s. He was a forward of outstanding skill and agility who won back-to-back European Cups with Brian Clough's Nottingham Forest. He joined them from Birmingham City as Britain's first £1m player. Later he tasted success with Sampdoria in Italy and Rangers in Scotland, and had a fruitful time managing Sheffield Wednesday in the early 90s, where he took the club to two cup finals and a third place in the final season of the old First Division. He also played 52 times for England, including at the 1982 World Cup in Spain. Fame and fortune came to Francis at an unusually young age, but it did not spoil him either as a player or a person. A universally popular figure, he was admired for his easygoing nature and humble approachability. As a player he oozed class. Far more than just a striker, he preferred to use his pace to run at defences. He also had a great passing ability as well as the knack of crossing balls at speed. Although he scored in excess of 230 goals during his career, occasionally he seemed more like an attacking midfielder than anything else. Francis retired to live in Marbella, Spain, where he died in 2023.

When Clough signed Francis, he insisted that the fee should be £999,999 so that the tag wouldn't go to the player's head, but after add-ons the fee was well in excess of a million.

 Jerome Allen 'Jerry' Seinfeld
born on 29th April 1954 in Brooklyn, New York City, USA

Jerry developed an interest in stand-up comedy while at college. After graduating in 1976, he performed at New York's 'Catch a Rising Star' open mic nights with only limited success. He continued performing in local clubs and Catskill Mountain resorts until his career was boosted by an appearance on a Rodney Dangerfield special. His career really took off when, in 1981, he landed a spot on *The Tonight Show Starring Johnny Carson*. This national recognition meant offers of work came flooding in. One of his early acting roles was that of Frankie in the highly popular TV comedy *Benson*, starring Robert Guillaume. This should have been a happy time, but after only four episodes Seinfeld was fired. After this chastening experience, he swore never to do another sitcom unless he had greater control. This opportunity emerged when he was invited to create a sitcom for NBC in 1989 where he teamed up with one-time stand-up colleague Larry David. What was originally *The Seinfeld Chronicles* morphed into simply *Seinfeld*. The show went on to be one of the most watched comedy shows in US television history. Seinfeld pulled the plug on his eponymous show in 1998. However, he still popped up, mainly playing himself, in shows such a Larry David's *Curb Your Enthusiasm* and *30 Rock*.

"There's very little advice in men's magazines, because men don't think there's a lot that they don't know. Women do. Women want to learn. Men think I know what I'm doing, just show me somebody naked."

Neil Francis Tennant
born on 10th July 1954 in North Shields, Tyne and Wear, UK

Tennant's first musical forays came in his teenage years in Newcastle with a folk band called Dust. His early songs were composed on guitar and inspired by whichever chord he had learned that day. The very first song he wrote, *Can You Hear the Dawn Break?* was a folk number which he was invited to perform on BBC Radio Newcastle. At the time he relied on his day job in publishing to make a living. In 1981, he edited Mary Berry's *ITV Cookbook*. It was around this time that Tennant met Chris Lowe in a music shop on the King's Road. They would spend their spare time listening to the pioneers of electronic music like Kraftwerk, Soft Cell and the Human League. With the help of producer Bobby Orlando they recorded *It's a Sin* and *Opportunities (Let's Make Lots of Money)*. The newly named Pet Shop Boys had truly arrived. Between 1983 and 1984 Orlando recorded a total of 11 tracks with Tennant and Lowe, including *West End Girls*. Despite gaining some airtime in France and the US, their music wasn't selling. They decided to part company with Orlando. When they teamed up with producer Stephen Hague later in 1984, their fortunes changed. A reworking of *West End Girls* became a worldwide hit and *In The Night* was used as the theme music for BBC's *Clothes Show*. The band would go on to sell more than 50 million records. Tennant was influential in pushing David Cameron's government to formally pardon the gay scientist and World War 2 code breaker Alan Turing in 2013, the centenary year of his birth.

Tennant cites T.S. Eliot and John Betjeman as his biggest influences.

Angela Dorothea Merkel (née Kasner)
born on 17th July 1954 in Hamburg, West Germany

Merkel is a prominent German politician who made a lasting impact on her country and international politics. She served as the Chancellor of Germany from 2005 to 2021, making her one of the longest-serving leaders in modern German history. Her political career began in the wake of the fall of the Berlin Wall in 1989 when she joined the Christian Democratic Union (CDU). She rose through the ranks, becoming the party's leader in 2000 and subsequently, the Chancellor. She was known for her pragmatic and cautious approach to politics, earning her the nickname 'Mutti' or 'Mother' among Germans. During her tenure, she steered Germany through various unique crises, including the global financial crash of 2008 and the Eurozone crisis. Her leadership was characterised by a commitment to the European Union, supporting financial stability and managing the refugee crisis in 2015, which involved welcoming a large number of refugees into Germany. Merkel's leadership style was characterised by her ability to maintain political stability, build consensus and negotiate with other European leaders. She was a key figure in international diplomacy, often mediating on global issues and working closely with leaders such as Barack Obama. Her tenure ended in 2021, with her stepping down as Chancellor. She remains a respected figure in global politics, known for her calm approach to leadership and her role as a unifying force in a changing world.

"Freedom does not mean being free of something, but to be free to do something."

James Francis Cameron CC
born on 16th August 1954 in Kapuskasing, Ontario, Canada

Cameron is a film director who can do 'big' better than any director since Cecil B. DeMille. But it was not always that way. He moved to the USA in 1971, where he chased his dream of becoming a screenwriter, taking a job as a truck driver to support his ambition. He landed his first professional film job as art director, miniature-set builder and process-projection supervisor on Roger Corman's *Battle Beyond the Stars* (1980). He had his first experience as a director with a two week stint on *Piranha Part Two: The Spawning* (1982) before being fired. He then wrote and directed *The Terminator* (1984), a futuristic action-thriller starring Arnold Schwarzenegger and Linda Hamilton. It was a low budget independent film, but Cameron's superb, dynamic direction made it a surprise mainstream success. It is now regarded as one of the most iconic pictures of the 1980s. After this came a string of successful, bigger budget science-fiction action films such as *Aliens* (1986), *The Abyss* (1989) and *Terminator 2: Judgement Day* (1991). In 1997, he wrote and directed *Titanic* which became the highest grossing movie of all time. 12 years later he would eclipse this record when *Avatar* (2009), which used pioneering 3D film technology, went on to beat *Titanic*. It was also the first film ever to cost more than two billion dollars to create. Cameron's films have grossed over $8 billion worldwide. Only Steven Speilberg's films have grossed more.

Cameron is also a famed deep sea explorer. He reached the bottom of the Mariana Trench on 25th March 2012, becoming the first person ever to do so in a one-man craft.

Elvis Costello born Declan Patrick MacManus
born on 25th August 1954 in London, England

Costello is the son of band leader Ross MacManus. He took his stage name from his idol Elvis Presley and his father's stage name Day Costello. He began performing professionally in 1969 and was a musician and singer in many bands around London before forming a moderately successful pub-rock band called 'Flip City' in the mid-1970s. Working full time as a computer operator, he landed his first record deal with Stiff Records in 1977 and recorded his first album *My Aim Is True* while on holiday. The album was a smash hit in the UK and landed Costello a worldwide distribution deal with Columbia records. Forming his backing group, The Attractions, for his second album, Costello went on to record several popular and influential albums over the next decade. Today, he is regarded as one of the most influential and popular singer/songwriters in modern music. In 1998, he collaborated with legendary tune smith, Burt Bacharach, on a highly successful album of love songs *Painted From Memory*. Throughout his career Costello has shown enormous versatility, writing pulsating rock songs, jazz, ballads, folk and country music. He has also written music for films such as Alan Bleasdale's Bafta award-winning miniseries *G.B.H.* (1991) and *The Shape of Things* (2003).

In 2017, Costello helped establish the Musician Treatment Foundation as a member of its board of directors. The foundation, which is based in Austin, Texas, helps under- and uninsured musicians receive free orthopaedic care for limb injuries.

Stuart Leslie Goddard aka Adam Ant
born on 3rd November 1954 in Marylebone, London, UK

Stuart Goddard's father had been in the Royal Air Force and worked as a chauffeur, while his mother was an embroiderer for leading fashion designer Norman Hartnell. After his parent's divorce, his mother worked as a cleaning lady for amongst others Paul McCartney. The combination of fashion and music clearly had an influence on Stuart as he morphed into Adam Ant. From 1977 to 1982 he performed with his backing group 'The Ants'. After approaching producer Malcolm McLaren to manage his band, McLaren instead took his backing band to form the group Bow Wow Wow. Adam started again with new members, and found huge success with his second album *Kings of the Wild Frontier* in 1980. In 1982, he quit the group for a solo career, keeping only Marco Pirroni as a band member and co-songwriter. By the end of the decade, his popularity had waned and he pursued an acting career, appearing in the TV series *Tales From the Crypt* and *Northern Exposure*. His music is his lasting legacy and between 1980 and 1983 he scored 10 UK top 10 hits, including three UK number one singles: *Stand and Deliver*, *Prince Charming* and *Goody Two Shoes*. Ant returned to music in 2010 and has subsequently completed many international tours. He released a new album in 2013.

Goddard renamed himself Adam Ant, because "I really knew I wanted to be Adam, because Adam was the first man. Ant I chose because, if there's a nuclear explosion, the ants will survive."

Ann 'Annie' Lennox
born on 25th December 1954 in Aberdeen, Scotland

Lennox, who was a gifted musician as a child, moved to London aged 17 to enrol at the Royal Academy of Music where she studied classical flute, piano and harpsichord. Although she later stated that she was proud to have studied at the college, she did not fit in and dropped out. In the late 1970s she was working in a vegetarian restaurant in Hampstead when she met Dave Stewart. The two would become romantically involved as well as forming the band The Catch which was soon renamed The Tourists. Only moderate success followed which put a strain on the pair's relationship. After disbanding The Tourists and ending their relationship, the two agreed to work together and formed The Eurythmics. Lennox's commanding stage presence, vocal versatility and androgynous style would go on to propel the pair to stardom. Their first album *In the Garden* (1981) was only moderately successful, leaving Lennox despondent. She channelled her frustrations into songwriting and produced *Sweet Dreams (Are Made of This)* (1983) which became the title track of their second album. The song reached number two on the UK charts and hit number one on the Billboard Hot 100 chart in the US. Since then, she has enjoyed great success both with the band and as a solo performer with such songs as *Love Song For a Vampire* (1993) and *No More 'I Love You's'* (1995). Lennox was inducted to the Songwriters Hall of Fame in 2020.

In 2008, Lennox founded The Circle of Women, known as The Circle, a charitable organisation to network and fund-raise for women's projects around the world.

Denzel Hayes Washington Jr.
born on 28th December 1954 in Mount Vernon, New York, USA

Washington first studied journalism at Fordham University but soon discovered an interest in acting. He made his feature film debut in the comedy *A Carbon Copy* (1981) and was cast in the hit TV medical drama *St. Elsewhere* (1982-88). He went on to appear in several hit movies including *Philadelphia* (1993), *Man on Fire* (2004), *The Book of Eli* (2010), *American Gangster* (2007) and *Flight* (2012). He won Oscars for his roles in *Glory* (1989) and *Training Day* (2001). He received an Oscar nomination for his starring role in 2016's *Fences*, an adaptation of August Wilson's Tony and Pulitzer Prize-winning play, and for the 2017 film *Roman J. Israel, Esq*. On stage Washington played the leading role in Lorraine Hansberry's *A Raisin in the Sun* on Broadway in 2014, to critical acclaim. Continuing his work on stage, he starred in the Broadway revival of *The Iceman Cometh* in 2018, playing Theodore 'Hickey' Hickman. His career defining role came in close friend and frequent collaborator Spike Lee's 3hr 22m epic *Malcolm X* (1992), where Washington played the lead. It left such a mark on him that he named one of his sons Malcolm. Throughout Washington's career he has probably played more civil rights activists and victims of injustice than any other actor, including South African Steve Biko in *Cry Freedom* (1987) and Ruben Carter in *The Hurricane* (1999).

Asked where he likes to keep his Oscars the ever confident, Washington replied "next to each other."

Other Notable Births

 Howard Stern
12th January 1954
Broadcaster

 Matt Groening
15th February 1954
Cartoonist | Animator

 Rene Russo
17th February 1954
Actress | Model

 Anthony Head
20th February 1954
Actor | Singer

 Ron Howard
1st March 1954
Filmmaker | Actor

 Jane Campion
30th April 1954
Filmmaker

 Jim Belushi
15th June 1954
Actor

 Kathleen Turner
19th June 1954
Actress

 Cherie Blair
23rd September 1954
Barrister | Writer

 Sam Allerdyce
19th October 1954
Football Manager

 Ang Lee
23rd October 1954
Filmmaker

 Lee Child
29th October 1954
Author

 Ross Brawn
23rd November 1954
F1 Team Principal

 Ray Liotta
18th December 1954
Actor

 Chris Evert
21st December 1954
Tennis Player

Sydney Hughes Greenstreet
died aged 74 on 18th January 1954 in Hollywood, California, USA

Greenstreet's father was a leather merchant with eight children. Sydney left England at age 18 to make his fortune as a Ceylon tea planter, but drought forced him out of business and back home. He managed a brewery and, to escape boredom, took acting lessons. His stage debut was as a murderer in a 1902 production of *Sherlock Holmes*. From then on he appeared in numerous plays in England and the US, working through most of the 1930s with Alfred Lunt and Lynn Fontanne at the Theatre Guild. His parts ranged from musical comedy to Shakespeare. His film debut, occurring when he was 62 years old and weighing nearly 300 pounds, was as Kasper Guttman in the classic *The Maltese Falcon* (1941) with Humphrey Bogart and Peter Lorre. He teamed up with Lorre in eight more movies after that including *Casablanca* (1942). In 8 years he made 24 films, all while beset by diabetes and Bright's disease. In 1949, ill heath forced his acting retirement.

Thomas William Pierrepoint
died aged 83 on 11th February 1954 in Bradford, West Riding, UK

There were no formal qualifications to become a hangman. Thomas Pierrepoint entered the profession through a family connection starting his life as an executioner on the recommendation of his brother Henry, who served as chief executioner from 1901-1910. By the outbreak of World War I he had his fingers in many pies. He ran a smallholding, carrier service and an illegal bookmakers, whilst always being on standby to carry out the death penalty. Thomas' career as a hangman resulted in his working in the role for 39 years, during which time he carried out 294 hangings, of which 203 were civilians executed in England and Wales. The other executions he conducted abroad and/or on military personnel. In 1940, his fitness for the job was questioned by a medical officer who called him "unsecure" and doubted "whether his sight was good". Thomas never officially retired, rather his name was removed from the list of executioners.

William Harrison Hays Sr.
died aged 74 on 7th March 1954 in Sullivan, Indiana, USA

After a career in politics, Hays became the first President of the Motion Picture Producers and Distributors Association of America. As Postmaster General, he had been an outspoken opponent of sending obscene materials through the post. Thus, when Hollywood's producers and studio heads decided to form their own watchdog organisation after several major scandals during the early 1920's (Arbuckle, Wallace Reed etc), they felt that Hays was perfect for the job. Beginning in 1922, and for more than two decades thereafter, it was a job that Hays took very seriously. He reached his peak with the adoption of the so-called, highly restrictive Hays Code in 1934. It not only restricted violent and sexual content, but famously the duration of an on-screen kiss. By the late 1940's, however, the US Supreme Court ruled that films were protected under the First Amendmen. From this point on, Hays felt his power starting to slip.

Magdalena Carmen Frida Kahlo y Calderón

died aged 47 on 13th July 1954 in Coyoacán, Mexico City, Mexico

Kahlo's work is marked by the vivid colours and symbolism of traditional Mexican art. She is famous for her persistent exploration of the female form and her self-representation through many introspective self-portraits. Her early life was marred by trauma. Aged six, she contracted polio so her mother bought her an easel which allowed her to paint whilst bed-ridden. When she was 18, she suffered life-changing injuries in a bus crash. These experiences greatly influenced her art as she became ever more introspective. It is no surprise that of her 142 or so paintings, 55 were self-portraits. In 1929 she married fellow artist Diego Rivera, who was 21 years her senior. Her mother opposed the marriage calling it "a marriage between an elephant and a dove", referring to the couple's differences in size. Rivera was tall and overweight while Kahlo was petite and fragile. Sorrow was never far away for Kahlo: "I drank to drown my sorrows, but the damned things learned how to swim."

Henri Émile Benoît Matisse

died aged 84 on 3rd November 1954 in Nice, France

Matisse was a French visual artist, known for both his use of colour and his fluid and original draughtsmanship. He was also a print maker and sculptor, but is known primarily as a painter. Matisse is commonly regarded, along with Pablo Picasso, as one of the artists who best helped to define the revolutionary developments in the visual arts throughout the opening decades of the twentieth century. He was responsible for significant developments in painting and sculpture. The intense colourism of the works he painted between 1900 and 1905 brought him renown as one of the Fauves (French for 'wild beasts'). Many of his finest works were created in the decade or so after 1906, when he developed a style that emphasised flattened forms and decorative pattern. In 1917, he relocated to a suburb of Nice on the French Riviera. The more relaxed style of his work during the 1920s gained him critical acclaim as an upholder of the classical tradition in French painting.

Enrico Fermi

died aged 53 on 28th November 1954 in Chicago, Illinois, USA

Enrico Fermi's early research was in general relativity and quantum mechanics, but he soon focused on the newer field of nuclear physics. He won the Nobel Prize in 1938 for his work on radioactivity, allowing him to escape fascist Italy and settle in the USA. Subsequently during World War II, Fermi became one of the principal leaders on the Manhattan Project, which focused on the development of the Atomic Bomb. To further his commitment to his new country, Fermi and his wife became American citizens in 1944. Although central to the creation of the Atomic Bomb, Fermi was a fierce critic of the development of the Hydrogen Bomb, which was 1,000 times more powerful than its predecessor. When President Truman ordered the development of the bomb, Fermi returned to his Los Alamos laboratory hoping to prove that making a super bomb wasn't possible; but to no avail. Element 100, Fermium, is named in his honour.

The Coins We Used

17 years before decimalisation, we used the system of pounds, shillings and pence commonly represented using the symbols **£sd**. The **£** symbol evolved over many years from the letter L which derives from the Latin word libra, meaning a pound of money. Although **s** is the first letter of the word shilling, the use of the letter derives from the Latin word *solidus* which means coin. The curious use of the letter **d** for pennies also has a Latin origin from the word *denarius* meaning containing ten. Unlike the decimal system based on multiples of 10, the pre-decimal system was based on multiples of 12. There were 12 pennies to a shilling and 240 pennies to a pound. This meant there were 20 shillings to the pound. In 1954 there were 9 coins in circulation with evocative names that still permeate our language today.

Farthing ¼ d
In use to 1961

With 4 farthings to a penny, these smallest of coins featured a smooth edge and a wren on the reverse. He hasn't got two farthings to rub together was a popular expression to describe someone poor.

Halfpenny ½ d
In use to 1969

Commonly known as the ha'penny it is was the only word in the English language with a silent 'f'. Since 1937 the coin featured Sir Francis Drake's ship The Golden Hind. The popular pub game Shove Ha'penny features 5 halfpennies.

Penny 1d
In use to 1971

Pre 1860 the penny was a large copper coin. This is why bicycles with a large front wheel were nicknamed Penny Farthings. Popular expressions using the penny include *ten a penny* and *penny for your thoughts*.

Threepence 3d
In use to 1971

These 12-sided coins were commonly known as *thruppence* or *thrupenny bits*. The silver versions known as joeys were often hidden in Christmas puddings making an exciting find for the lucky children who discovered them.

Sixpence 6d
In use to 1980

These silver coins reputedly brought good luck. Sixpences were placed in bride's shoes as a wedding gesture. Known as benders, they could easily be bent. *Going on a bender* derived from drinking all day in pubs with sixpence.

Shilling 1/-
In use to 1990

First minted in the reign of Henry VII as a testoon, the shilling was latterly commonly known as a bob. *Taking the king's shilling* meant enrolling in the army whilst *A few bob short of a pound* describes someone a bit mad.

Florin 2/-
In use to 1992

The florin was Britain's first decimal coin in response to calls in the mid 19th century for decimal coinage to be introduced. As 2 *bob* the florin was worth 1/10th of a pound. After decimalisation in 1971 florins became worth 10 pence.

Half Crown 2/6
In use to 1969

Half crowns were originally struck in gold in the reign of Henry VIII. The first silver half crowns were issued under Edward VII in 1557. Surviving for over 450 years, the Half Crown was one of the most successful coins of all time.

Crown 5/-
In use to present day

The British crown is a heavy silver coin. Rarely spent crowns are often minted for commemorative purposes. After decimalisation a crown was worth 25p until 1990 when their face value was changed to £5.

The average annual salary in the UK in 1954 was approximately:

£375 - £500

The Ford Anglia was sold in the UK between 1939 and 1967. Over 1.5 million Anglia's were produced before being replaced by the Ford Escort. In 1954, this 3rd generation Ford Anglia 100E model would have cost:

£511

The price of the average house would be approximately 5-6x the average annual wage. Depending on where you were in the country, this meant the price of a typical 1930's 3-bedroom semi-detached house would be in the region of:

£1800 - £2500

The Bush TV22 television set had an iconic Bakelite design holding a 9" screen receiving only one channel. Very expensive for the average family, they cost:

£38 12s

In 1954, the average price of a large wholemeal loaf of bread was:

7½d

A gallon of petrol (which is equivalent to 4.5 litres) cost:

4s 6½d

National Service

National service recruits enjoying a cup of tea whilst off duty in a NAAFI

Indian and British soldiers in Korea

National Service was introduced in 1947 to overcome challenges and resolve military manpower shortages in the wake of World War II. Wartime conscription was extended into an obligatory period of National Service for men of military age. Over 2 million were called up to the armed forces, often serving in one of Britain's many colonial outposts around the world.

After passing a medical and joining up, all conscripts had six weeks of basic training during which they got used to military life. Once enlisted and inside camp, National Servicemen were issued with their equipment which often consisted of ill-fitting uniforms and boots. Conscripts were knocked into shape by sergeants under pressure to train them in as short a time as possible. Most conscripts lived in cold barracks with primitive toilets and washing facilities. The lucky few had newly built, brick barracks with central heating. Some were housed in a 'Barrack Spider', a wooden hut with eight rooms and a central washing area. Up to twenty men were housed in each room. Each man had a steel wardrobe, an iron bed and a one-foot locker for small items of kit. Overseas accommodation varied a lot. Servicemen could find themselves sharing a tent with three other men such as in camps in Cyprus, or even as many as 15 as in war-torn Korea.

The camps and accommodation for servicemen in the Suez Canal zone were amongst the worst, but those in Germany were generally of a high standard. Recruits soon began the seemingly endless task of polishing kit and equipment. Many regarded this as mindless drill aimed at destroying individuality. However, this strict regime helped foster a group identity and brought recruits closer together with many lifelong friendships being formed. Officers who did four years or more on a Short Service Commission were allowed to train in a speciality. Many other ranks were trained in general clerical duties, such as typing. Some received more specific training in technical subjects, such as communications and engineering. Languages were also taught at the Joint Service School of Languages at Bodmin. Russian was especially useful in this Cold War era. For those stationed in war zones, the possibility of death was suddenly part of daily life. The experience many men had of being thrown into combat situations, such as in Korea, Malaysia and Egypt, would never be forgotten. Men with minimal training were expected to fight hardened guerrilla fighters or cope with riots or civil unrest. Between 1947 and 1963, a total of 395 National Servicemen were killed on active duty.

Office Life

The first thing that would strike you if you were transported back to a British office in 1954, is that there was very little plugged in to the wall. Virtually everything from typewriters to adding machines were manual. In large offices, the typing pool, which was almost universally staffed by women, was a noisy place. Correcting mistakes was done either by correction fluid or a ribbon, which necessitated the typist using a backspace key and retyping the offending letter or word thereby masking it. Often, letters would look a bit of a mess so accuracy was highly prized. Secretarial training was considered a good move for young women and gave them an income and financial freedom.

A state of the art office environment in 1954

An employee creating punch cards

For many it was a job to do before marriage and domestic life, and it was always a good skill to have as it gave them "something to fall back on". After marriage, work as a school secretary was sought after as it allowed married woman to continue working in the knowledge that their hours and holidays coincided with their children's. There were virtually no computers, in fact the term was more likely to describe a person than it was a machine. The photocopier, invented in the US, was still in development and was virtually no use at all. One copy would take up to fifteen minutes to produce, meaning that it was often quicker to have a secretary type the letter again. Larger offices were very regimented places. The managers, nearly all men, would have separate toilet facilities, dining rooms and in some places even lifts. The general staff, consisting of mainly female secretaries, maintenance men and messenger boys shared the general staff canteen, which was often a more fun place to be.

The glass ceiling for women, except in very rare cases, was reached when usually a more mature woman became a personal secretary to a manager. Along with all general clerical duties, she was charged with running the manager's schedule, organising and laying out meetings, attending to the diary, answering phone calls and especially on a Friday after many a manager had a liquid lunch, telling people that her boss was "currently indisposed". It would take decades for the British office to become more egalitarian places where staff were not employed on the basis of gender or the colours of an old school tie.

Secretaries hard at work in the typing pool

Life on the Farm

Farm machinery replaced work originally done by labourers

A family on their summer break helping with the harvest

Farming in Britain was in a state of great flux in 1954. A new age of mechanisation was dawning as the country emerged from the war years. Back then, the call to "Dig for Victory" encouraged food production on every spare acre of land. Even in 1954, nine years after the end of the war, food shortages still prevailed with farming strictly controlled by the Government. The Journal of the Ministry of Agriculture announced that "The world food outlook is very grave indeed....a united effort on the part of scientists and farmers will be needed if the situation is to be saved". Farmers quickly noted that the ministry mentioned scientists first with this causing tension between those who worked the land and those who told them how to do it. Through subsidy and control the government encouraged the production of arable crops, milk, pork and eggs. This led to a marked increase in the price of other produce with food shortages still prevalent. Although mechanisation helped with the workload, most work was done by hand.

The life of a farm labourer was tough. Ploughing and harvesting were increasingly done by machine but such tasks as milking cows, digging drainage channels and bailing hay were done by hand. Farmers, as they do today, largely lived by the hours of daylight; harvest time in the Autumn was particularly arduous. In the summertime when fruit was at its most bountiful, families and teenage children travelled from the towns and cities to help with the harvest. A hangover from this persists to this day; it is the reason children are given six weeks' summer holiday. However, British children should have been thankful that they did not grow up in Ireland where they had three months "holiday".

Famously, London schoolchildren were sent by coach to Kent to help with hop picking for the brewing industry. Many had fond memories of the experience, but most often living conditions were poor, pay was minimal and some yearned for the relative tranquillity of home and even school! For farmers the highlight of the year, as it is today, was the country show. This was and is an age old celebration of all things rural. There were dances, food aplenty, tug of war contests between the rufty-tufty farmhands and the quaffing of large amounts of the local brew. These were also places where business was done and contests for the best livestock often resulted in the winner changing hands for a princely sum.

The Primary School

In 1954 there were no state funded nurseries. For most children their early life centred around the home, cared for by a stay-at-home mother or other members of their extended family. Children entered school at the age of five and for many it was a big shock. Tears were often shed at the school gates as mothers loosened their grip both literally and metaphorically. The day would start with assembly and a roll-call, the register. Children would sit cross-legged on the floor and listen to an address from the headteacher which was followed by the singing of a hymn. It was then on to the classroom.

A game of marbles in the playground

A lesson in how to hold the bat

Each pupil was assigned their own desk, this normally faced the front of the classroom. The desk had a flap with storage space underneath and an inkwell at its upper edge. Children were eased gently into school life and little was done on the first day. Upon returning home, many were surprised to find out that they had to do it again the next day. When lessons became serious there was much emphasis on the "three Rs": reading, writing and arithmetic. This immediately confused many as only one of the subjects actually began with R. Reading often involved reciting poetry or prose from memory or reading passages of a book aloud. Writing was not only a test of spelling and grammar, but also of handwriting skills. Pupils normally wrote in pencil except when they were taught rudimentary calligraphy. Some fared better than others and the skills learned stayed with them through to adulthood.

For others it was torture as each pupil was at the mercy of the children who had used the nib pen before them. Each pen was worn down in different ways and this bias was particularly difficult for left-handers. Arithmetic (maths) involved learning the times table, usually up to the number 12. The Britain of the day was pre-decimal and had 12 pennies to a shilling so knowing how to count in twelves was useful. There were few gizmos, the teacher stood at the front of the class and wrote on a blackboard. The pupils would have little more than a geometry set consisting of a set square, a protractor, a metal compass, a pencil and sharpener and a stencil. Other than the pencil, most items were rarely used.

There was also music and movement, and gym. Music and movement encouraged free expression, but most pupils of the day can only remember being asked to pretend that they were a tree swaying in the wind. Gym involved vaulting and climbing over a mini assault course. This was a hangover from military training during the war and was performed in underwear. Eleven was a crucial age for children as they had to sit the Eleven-plus exam. Very often it would shape the rest of their lives. If you passed you went to a grammar school, failure would see you go to a secondary modern or technical college.

Children at a primary school in Wales

Background

After the Second World War, the state funded secondary education system was divided using a Tripartite system containing grammar schools, secondary technical colleges and secondary modern schools. The Eleven-plus examination was used to select which pupils went to which schools based on ability. As technical colleges were not available on the scale envisaged, the exam came to symbolise fierce competition for places at the prestigious grammar schools. The very name still deeply divides opinion with many believing it was the symbol of a segregated two-tier school system whilst for others it set the educational benchmark.

Here's your chance to test yourself with example questions from the 1950s:
(Answers on page 92)

Arithmetic Questions

Question One: A motorist who left home at 11.15am, drives at 36 miles per hour. He stops for lunch from 1.15pm to 2.45pm and then continues his journey at 40 miles per hour. How many miles in total has he travelled by 6pm?

Question Two: 785 is multiplied by 50 and the result is divided by 125. Write down the answer.

Question Three: A ship uses 200 gallons of diesel for a voyage of 300 miles. How far could it travel using 80 gallons?

Question Four: Write in figures the sum of three hundred and seventy six and eighty-nine.

Question Five: Elizabeth is 8 years old and her father is 38. Answer the following:

A) How old was Elizabeth's father when he was 6 times as old as her?

B) In how many years' time will her father be three times as old as Elizabeth?

C) How old will Elizabeth be when her father becomes 15 times as old as she was 4 years ago?

General Intelligence Questions

Question One: Each of the following jumbled sentences can make sense by interchanging two words. Rewrite the sentences:

A) A was stung by Billy bee.

B) The shepherd whistled by the gate and stood to his dog.

C) The swim went to the pool for a family.

Question Two: The letters PELAP are the letters of the word APPLE jumbled up. Rearrange the following:

A) TOUNOCC is a fruit which comes from abroad.

B) FARFIGE is a large animal.

C) TIPACRAI is a girl's name.

Question Three: Each of the following sentences contains one error. Rewrite the sentences correctly:

A) When the dog saw me, it wagged it's tail.

B) The subject doesn't concern you or I.

C) Whilst speaking to my brother, the police car past me.

Top 10 Girls' Baby Names [1]

1. Susan — of Hebrew origin meaning "Lily Rose"
2. Linda — from the German for *lime tree* via Spanish where it meant "Pretty"
3. Christine — of Latin and French origin meaning "Follower of Christ"
4. Margaret — from *Margarita*, the Old Persian name meaning "Pearl"
5. Janet — of Old English origin meaning "God's gracious gift"
6. Patricia — derived from the Latin word *Patrician* meaning "Noble"
7. Carol — originally an Old German man's name meaning "Freeman"
8. Elizabeth — of Hebrew origin meaning "God is my oath"
9. Mary — from Latin meaning "Star of the sea"
10. Anne — of Hebrew origin meaning "The gracious one"

Top 10 Boys' Baby Names [2]

1. David — corruption of the Hebrew name *Dawid* meaning "beloved"
2. John — of Hebrew origin meaning "God is Gracious"
3. Stephen — of Greek origin meaning "Garland or crown"
4. Michael — of Hebrew origin meaning "One who is like God"
5. Peter — of Greek and biblical origin meaning "Rock"
6. Robert — from Old German meaning "Bright Fame"
7. Paul — from Latin meaning "Small" or "Humble"
8. Alan — from the Celtic for "Harmony" or "Noble"
9. Christopher — of Greek origin meaning "Bearer of Christ"
10. Richard — from Old German meaning "Powerful leader"

[1] [2] Data compiled by the Office for National Statistics 1954

1954 | A Sweet Renaissance

In 1954, the confectionery industry was booming following the end of post-World War II rationing in 1953. The post-war economic recovery saw disposable income rising leading to a surge in demand for confectionery items. Chocolate, which had been a luxury during the war years, once again became widely available and immensely popular. Iconic brands such as Cadbury and Rowntree's were at the forefront of the market. One significant trend was the innovation in chocolate bar varieties. Cadbury, for instance, expanded its range with products that are now classics like the Dairy Milk bar. The decade also witnessed the introduction of various candies and chewing gums, catering to a younger audience that had more spending power than before. Bright, attractive packaging became more common, and advertising campaigns became increasingly sophisticated often targeting children and families. This was a time when television was becoming more widespread, offering new opportunities for advertising. The confectionery industry in the UK in 1954 was characterised by a mix of innovation, expansion, and nostalgia. Traditional sweets like Liquorice Allsorts and Sherbet Lemons remained popular, while new products continually entered the market, reflecting a nation eager to indulge in the sweeter things in life after years of austerity.

At the start of 1954 certain foods were still being rationed following the war, so the evening meal would often be a simple affair. Meat rationing ended in July 1954 which came as a welcome relief to many families. Refrigeration was still a luxury most could not afford, so food would often be bought daily.

Pictured is Margaret Jones at her home in North Wales. She is collecting a plate of homemade butter from the scullery ready for the evening meal.

Mr. Davidson is seen writing a letter to his sister who lives in the United States. Writing bureaus were sought after pieces of furniture in the 1950s, often being passed down the generations as family heirlooms.

Relaxing in their armchairs in the front room of their house are teachers Mr. and Mrs. Samuel from Ebbw Vale. To the right is the tiled fireplace, a focal point for the family to gather around. The hearth is also a particular favourite for the family cat, Shan.

Dick Parry, toy maker, shows some of his Christmas toys to his children at the family home in Shrewsbury. Toy trains and doll houses featured heavily on the Christmas lists of fifties children.

Lucienne Day, pictured here, with her Calyx fabric pattern. This design generated a new school of pattern-making which became known as the 'Contemporary' style.

The Birth of Modern Design

By the 1950s Britain was slowly emerging from the privations of the Great Depression of the 1930s and from the 1940s which were overshadowed by war and its resultant shortages. The 1950s slowly became the age of the consumer and in the home it was very much "out with the old and in with the new". The 1950s was also an age when the political parties competed with each other to build new public housing. The Prime Minister Winston Churchill summoned the Housing Minister, Harold Macmillan, and tasked him with matching the previous Labour Government's achievement of building 200,000 new homes each year. These houses were smaller than pre-war homes, so furniture had to stack or be light enough to move around. Earlier inventions like serving trolleys, collapsible ironing boards and sofa beds became more commonplace. Nowhere could change be better seen than in the kitchen. Cottage style kitchens were replaced with sleek new fitted kitchens. For many, the pantry was replaced by a refrigerator for the first time.

The 1950s were also a time of great design. The most enduring furniture was created by the husband and wife team of Charles and Ray Eames who produced stylish plywood, plastic and leather furniture. Another husband and wife team who brought elegance and colour into the home were Robin and Lucienne Day. Lucienne was the most influential British textile designer of the age. Her most famous design, Calyx (pictured above), was created as a furnishing fabric and was used on the furniture designed by her husband. It was an abstract pattern composed of cup-shaped motifs joined by spindly lines and is one of the most recognisable and iconic designs of the 1950s.

Coronation Chicken

Coronation Chicken was a dish created to mark the coronation of Queen Elizabeth II the year before in 1953. It was a variation of Jubilee Chicken, which was created for the Silver Jubilee of George V in 1935. The dish consists of cold cooked chicken, which is usually poached, combined with a creamy mayonnaise-based sauce that contains Indian spices, such as curry powder and dried fruit like raisins. It is typically served as a sandwich filling, salad ingredient, or as part of a cold buffet. The dish was created by Constance Spry, an English food writer and Rosemary Hume, a chef. It was originally served at the reception following the coronation ceremony. The dish was intended to showcase the best of British cuisine, while also incorporating elements of Indian cuisine, which was fashionable at the time due to the British Empire's long history with India. The dish quickly gained popularity becoming a staple of British cuisine, appearing in many cookbooks and restaurants. It is still very popular today and is often served at picnics, buffets and other casual gatherings.

A recipe for classic Coronation Chicken (Serves 6)

Ingredients

- 1 medium sized chicken (around 3-4lbs)
- 1 pint and a half chicken stock (or enough to cover the chicken)
- 1 onion, chopped
- 1 bay leaf
- 3 teaspoons curry powder
- 6oz mayonnaise
- 2oz plain yogurt (or 8oz of mayonnaise if yogurt is unavailable)
- 2 tablespoons apricot jam (or mango chutney if available)
- 2 tablespoons lemon juice
- 3 oz cup raisins
- Salt and pepper, to taste

Method: Poach the chicken in the chicken stock with the onion and bay leaf until cooked through, about 60-80 mins. Remove from heat and let cool. In a small bowl, mix together the curry powder, mayonnaise, yogurt, apricot jam or mango chutney, lemon juice and raisins. Skin and bone the chicken and cut into bite-sized pieces and mix with the sauce. Season with salt and pepper. Chill in the refrigerator until ready to serve. Serve over a bed of greens or as a sandwich filling. Garnish with chopped parsley, if desired. **Enjoy!**

Pineapple Upside-Down Cake

Puddings were an essential part of dinner time in 1950s Britain, with some remembered more fondly than others. Jam roly-poly, tapioca, semolina, rice pudding, stewed fruit and custard or just plain old jelly and ice cream; all could follow the main meal. For something fancier, perhaps when having guests or family to dinner, a pineapple upside down cake made for a spectacular centrepiece. Tinned pineapples rings were relatively cheap and the number used was governed by the number in the tin. Small tins had 4 rings, large tins 7 or 8.

A recipe for Pineapple Upside-Down Cake (Serves 8)

Ingredients

For the cake:
7 pineapple rings (tinned)
7 glacé cherries
4oz softened butter
4oz caster or demerara sugar
2 large eggs or 3 small ones
4oz self raising flour
¼ teaspoon vanilla extract (optional)

For the sauce:
2oz butter, plus extra for greasing
3oz caster or demerara sugar

Method: Preheat the oven to gas mark 4/ 350 F. Lightly grease the baking tin. Melt 2oz butter and 3oz sugar in a pan and stir until combined. Pour the mixture into the tin, then arrange the pineapple rings on top, popping a cherry into the centre of each ring. Beat the remaining butter and sugar together until light and fluffy. Then beat in the eggs one at a time, beating well with each addition. Add a tablespoon of flour with the second egg (or third one if you are using small ones). Beat in the vanilla extract (if using) then fold in the remaining flour. Spoon the mixture carefully into the cake tin and spread evenly over the pineapple and cherries. Bake in the centre of the oven for 35 minutes or until the cake is springy to the touch Allow the cake to cool in the tin for five minutes before turning out onto a plate. Serve warm with cream, ice cream or custard. **Delicious!**

Undaunted by the situation these pocket-sized models are demonstrating the latest look for children at a fashion show.

Although introduced in the mid-1940s, the modern bikini was still very controversial and met with considerable social resistance. However in the early 1950s, stars such as Brigitte Bardot played a large part in bringing the bikini into the mainstream.

Ladies wearing lavish ball gowns, two with intricate embroidered floral patterns.

This elegant dress is set off with a fitted black waist belt and matching shoes.

Three types of beach/ nautical themed summer dresses. Geometric patterns would became a 1950s design hallmark.

On location in Switzerland, film star Audrey Hepburn is pictured wearing a popular linen dress style with the fashionable tight fitting waist belt.

The 1950's saw the rise of the sports jacket or sports coat for men. These patterned jackets were designed to be worn without matching trousers. Corduroy, suede, leather, denim and tweed were popular fabrics.

Father and son modelling formal coats for the winter. Trousers were loose fitting whilst Homburg hats remained popular.

The Great British Seaside Holiday

Thanks to the Holiday With Pay Act of 1938, Britons were allowed an annual paid holiday, although this gave them a measly week off per year. In 1954, those working in factories would often all have to take their holidays at the same time as production was halted in the summer. Better employers gave their workers two weeks. Only one in fifteen people ventured abroad, as few had the means to afford foreign travel. Popular destinations were those that could be reached by ferry such as France, Ireland, Holland and Belgium, although visitors to Ireland were swollen by the Irish population in Britain going home to visit family.

Relaxing by the swimming pool

A day trip to the seaside was very popular

Italy was a popular longer haul destination, but this would normally involve a flight, which would double the cost of the holiday. So for most a holiday meant one thing, a train journey to the Great British seaside, which was in its heyday. There were three main options as to where to stay. First, the guest house, with its list of rules about breakfast time and when you could use your room. Secondly, there were many holiday camps, some of which occupied old army barracks left over from the war. Camps such as Butlin's offered entertainment for both children and adults.

There was sandcastle building and sports and games such as tug-of-war and the three-legged races for the children. For adults, there were sports and dancing. There were also competitions for the adults, including Miss Lovely Legs and Mr. Knobbly Knees. The third and most cost-effective option was to stay with a relative, usually an older family member who had retired to live by the coast. Much time was spent on the beach, if the weather allowed. In the 1950s people did not think of using sunblock and the aim was to get as tanned as possible as fast as possible.

Messing around in the diving competition

A bucket and spade holiday

Very often tanning accelerators were used and were homemade concoctions. One such potion was created by mixing vegetable oils with puréed carrots. In order to get and show off your tan, bathing costumes were needed. Women were increasingly sporting a bikini, a two-piece swimsuit which had been designed by the Parisian fashion house of Jacques Heim. Men would sport shorts or trunks. Many children of the era have strong memories of wearing knitted woollen costumes, often created by a generous auntie. This would act like a sponge when the children entered the water and then get filled with sand on the beach. Upon drying they would then take on the composition of cement and become extremely uncomfortable.

Father Christmas arrives by train to hand out presents to an awaiting gathering of families

Two excited children opening their presents with their mother and grandfather watching over

Christmas and Hogmanay 1954

In Scotland the celebration of Christmas was muted in the 1950s. A dispute between the Calvinist Church of Scotland and the Catholic Church of Rome saw Christmas celebrations effectively banned for 400 years. Shops were not decorated; even Christmas trees and decorations in the home were few and far between. The fact that Christmas Day did not become a public holiday until 1958, meant the day was much like any other in Scotland. The Scots instead saved all their revelry for the New Year's Hogmanay. There were several traditions and superstitions that had to be taken care of before midnight. The house had to be cleaned and ashes from the fire taken out on New Years Eve. At the stroke of midnight someone, usually a dark haired man, would bring coal, shortbread and possibly a wee dram of whisky into the house, in a tradition known as first-footing. Then the party would well and truly begin with a rendition of Robert Burns' *Auld Lang Syne*. South of the border Christmas was celebrated with more gusto. Houses were adorned with trees and paper chains, which were often homemade. Christmas cards from relatives, neighbours and friends would be hung on string. Many would contain letters and might be the only written communication all year.

The celebrations in 1954 were particularly special as Christmas Day fell on a Saturday, meaning that the combined holiday of that and Boxing Day gave those who did not work at weekends a four day break. Christmas Eve was a time of particular excitement for children. They were encouraged to go to their beds by the promise of a visit from Father Christmas, and a mince pie and an alcoholic beverage were put out for him in preparation of his arrival. Many over-excited children slept with one eye open and noticed that Father Christmas bore more than a passing resemblance to their own father. They would wake up in the morning to the sight of a Christmas stocking or a pillow case, which contained assorted presents and the ubiquitous satsuma. As today, the Christmas dinner took centre stage. Turkey had not yet become the meat of choice and chicken was too expensive. Instead, beef was a staple for most. Britain was still in a time of austerity and many people grew their own vegetables, so the trimmings were abundant and of high nutritional value. The dinner was usually timed to finish before or start after the Queen's Speech. This was her second Christmas speech since her coronation. Her pre-recorded broadcast was heard on radio only at 3pm (it was first televised in 1957) and families would gather round and listen in silence to Her Majesty.

1954 was a good year for music. Although the UK charts were dominated by American acts such as Frankie Laine, Guy Mitchell and Doris Day, British male tenor vocalist David Whitfield became the first British artist to have a number one on both sides of the Atlantic with his rendition of *Cara Mia* (*My Beloved* in Italian). The year also saw the birth of Rock 'n' Roll. Sure, Rock and Roll had existed before, but the first documented use of the term replacing 'and' with 'n' came when American disc jockey Al Freed promoted his Rock 'n' Roll Jubilee at St. Nicholas Arena in New York City. The music genre was not new, most of the acts looked out of touch with the younger generation. One of the biggest hits of the year was Bill Haley and his Comets' *Rock Around the Clock*. Although Haley was around thirty at the time, his conservative manner and attire made him seem like a performer from a bygone

Bill Haley and his Comets

age. Step forward a certain Elvis Presley. In July, a somewhat shy Elvis recorded his first single at Sun Records with the A-side *That's All Right (Mama)* and the B-side *Blue Moon of Kentucky*. By the end of the month he had made a guest appearance on the Slim Whitman Show and a new kind of Rock 'n' Roll was born. The year also saw two singers-turned-actors being recognised. Ol' Blue Eyes Frank Sinatra won best supporting actor for his role in *From Here to Eternity* at the 26th Academy Award ceremony. Bing Crosby was also nominated for best actor for *The Country Girl*. Alfred Hitchcock's *Dial M for Murder* may not have set the world on fire upon release but *Rear Window,* his second film of 1954, was a huge box office success. Both starred Grace Kelly. On the small screen, the year saw the debut of *The Grove Family*, a rather mundane

Alfred Hitchcock

soap opera of the everyday life of a lower-middle class family from the London suburb of Hendon. The highlight of the first episode sees the Groves paying off their final mortgage payment. Further episodes demonstrated the importance of home security. The theme music for the series which ran until 1957, was composed by Eric Spear who went on to become better known as the composer of the theme tune to the long-running soap opera *Coronation Street*. The musical debut of the year happened on Broadway with a production of Harold Rome's *Fanny*. Audiences were treated to what would in Britain have been described as a kitchen sink drama. Fanny discovers she is pregnant out of wedlock and, under pressure from her mother, marries an older man who seeks an heir to his estate. The play opened in the West End in 1956 and starred Robert Morley. A lesser known musical, *The Girl in the Pink Tights*, ended up having a more interesting history. Marilyn Monroe refused to act in a film version in defiance of her studio contract, describing the play as "trash". Her refusal may also have had something to do with the fact that she was offered about a third of her co-star Frank Sinatra's fee.

Marilyn Monroe pictured in 1954

Rear Window

Directed by Alfred Hitchcock
Starring James Stewart, Grace Kelly and Raymond Burr
Premiered on 1st September 1954

Alfred Hitchcock's second film with James Stewart is the story of Stewart's enforced idleness due to a broken leg. He's an active man, a news photographer who constantly pushes himself into dangerous situations to get a picture. Idleness for him is pure torture. Fortunately or unfortunately as things turn out, he has a Greenwich Village apartment with a rear window that allows him to look in on his neighbours across the courtyard. It's like watching about 15 different soap operas at once. And with his photographic equipment including a zoom telephoto lens, Stewart gets himself involved with the various soap opera plots. He also has a girlfriend in Lisa Fremont (Grace Kelly).Kelly is playing a part that is really no stretch for her, a Park Avenue chic and rich woman who's really had quite the life of comfort. Stewart doesn't think she's ready for his kind of life and they have a running quarrel. That is until Stewart comes to the conclusion from observing one of the apartments that salesman Raymond Burr has killed his wife. Although he can't convince his detective friend Lt. Doyle (Wendell Corey), he does slowly convince his girlfriend and his nurse (Thelma Ritter) of the validity of his conclusion. *Rear Window* was remade for TV with Christopher Reeve, who had been paralysed in a riding accident, playing the lead role. The supporting cast included Daryl Hannah and Robert Foster.

A Star Is Born

Directed by George Cukor
Starring Judy Garland and James Mason
Released on 29th September 1954

The film charts the rise of Esther Blodgett (Garland) from band singer to Hollywood star. When drunken actor Norman Maine (Mason) staggers onto the stage during her performance for a crowd of Hollywood elite, she incorporates the intrusion into her act and saves him from further embarrassment. A grateful Maine introduces her to the head of a film studio. Blodgett changes her name to Vicki Lester at the behest of the studio and, after appearing in a hit musical, her career skyrockets. The two performers fall in love and marry, but their union is tested by Maine's declining career and chronic alcoholism. Director Cukor had filmed this tragedy twice before, as *What Price Hollywood?* (1932), and in 1937 it was shot again as *A Star Is Born*. Garland, who had appeared in an earlier radio version of the story, was refused financing for an updated film version by MGM. So she and husband Sidney Luft formed their own production company and obtained the funding from Warner Brothers. Garland's performance in the 1954 film is widely regarded as her greatest. The soundtrack relied heavily on earlier Gershwin numbers like *Swanee*, *The Man That Got Away* and *Its A New World*. The film was remade in 1976 with Barbra Streisand and Kris Kristofferson in the leads. A further remake was released in 2018 starring Lady Gaga and Bradley Cooper.

Doctor in the House

Directed by Ralph Thomas
Starring Dirk Bogarde, Kenneth More, Kay Kendall and Donald Sinden
Released on 23rd March 1954

Dirk Bogarde

Dirk Bogarde was at the height of his matinée idol handsomeness when he found himself playing the part of a new medical student at St. Swithin's Hospital, in the first of seven *Doctor* films. The story concerns the high jinks of the young medical students as they flirt with the nurses, attempt to pass their exams (sometimes more than once), drink and party. Bogarde is Simon Sparrow, the naive, serious-minded young man who comes into this den of playboys. All the cast are excellent, especially James Robertson Justice as Sir Lancelot Spratt, a role he truly made his own. The part was originally to be played by Robert Morley, but he demanded a payment of £15,000 (one quarter of the film's total budget) up front and this was rejected. Bogarde, as always, injects some shyness and gentleness into the proceedings; his scene with a new young mother when he delivers her baby is especially poignant. Bogarde had a very interesting career path; he wasn't really interested in being a 'movie star'. He worked his way into character parts finally working with directors like Luchino Visconti in prestigious, if not widely distributed, films. He also had a very prolific writing career, producing seven autobiographies and memoirs as well as six novels.

The Belles Of St. Trinian's

Directed by Frank Launder
Starring Alistair Sim, Joyce Grenfell and George Cole
Released on 28th September 1954

Alistair Sim

In a cast headed by the superb Alistair Sim who plays Miss Fritton the headmistress and her brother, race shark Clarence. We also find Joyce Grenfell as a policewoman joining the staff undercover (and no one was better than Grenfell at this jolly hockey sticks kind of stuff). Beryl Reid is a drunken chemistry teacher, Hermione Baddeley and Irene Handl play memorably unsuitable members of staff. George Cole plays 'flash' Harry, an odd-job man who deals with the export of the St. Trinian's bathtub gin and places racing bets for the girls. The incomparable Richard Wattis plays a harassed Ministry of Education inspector. The girls themselves include some memorable turns including Vivienne Martin as chain-smoking Bella and Belinda Lee as horny Amanda. Barbara Windsor and Carol White are also among the mix. The plot revolves around a race horse, Arab Boy, who ends up in the fourth-formers' dormitory. *The New York Times* wrote, "Credit Alastair Sim with doing excellently by the dual roles he assays...Joyce Grenfell makes a properly gangling, awkward and gullible lady sleuth; George Cole does a few delightful turns as the conniving Cockney go-between and last, but not least, the 'Belles of St. Trinian's' rate a vote of confidence for the whacky freedom of expression they exhibit. They all help make St. Trinian's a wonderfully improbable and often funny place to visit."

The Seven Samurai

Directed by Akira Kurosawa
Starring Toshirô Mifune and Takashi Shimura
Released on 26th April 1954

In the 16th century in Japan, a poor village is frequently looted by armed bandits who steal their crops. Their patriarch advises the villagers to hire a Ronin (a wandering samurai who has no lord and master) to defend their village. Four farmers head to town to seek out their possible protector, but they can offer just three meals of rice per day and lodging for the samurai. They succeed in hiring the warm-hearted veteran Kambei Shimada (Shimura) who advises that they need six other samurai to protect their lands. Kambei recruits the necessary five samurai and the brave jester Kikuchiyo (Mifune) and moves to the village. After a tense reception, Kambei plots a defence strategy and the samurai start training the farmers in how to defend their lands and families for the battle that approaches. The denouement is Kurosawa at his best. The acting is outstanding by everyone involved from the main characters all the way down to the very last extra. The camera use is brilliant and every scene is visually balanced. *The Seven Samurai* has had a huge influence on Western cinema, from *The Magnificent 7* (1960) (which is virtually a re-make) through to *A Bug's Life* (1998). The film is also the first one to use 'the wipe' as a way of changing from one scene to another. This technique was later used by George Lucas in his *Star Wars* movies. BBC Culture ranks it as the greatest foreign language film of all time.

Charles Laughton

Hobson's Choice

Directed by David Lean
Starring Charles Laughton, John Mills and Brenda de Banzie
Released on 19th April 1954

Hobson's Choice starts with dopey Will Mossop being awakened by feisty spinster Maggie Hobson from dreams of moving from the Salford cobblers' shop where he works, to a great shop in St Ann's Square, Manchester. She is the daughter of the hard-drinking, tight-fisted Hobson, pillar of the community and Will's boss. John Mills plays Will with the right amount of bewilderment and determination, at turns touching and hilarious while Brenda de Banzie gives Maggie a sense of desperation throughout her scheme to make 'her man' a success. The great Yorkshire actor Charles Laughton is superb as Hobson. Eagle-eyed TV fans will spot Prunella Scales (Sybil from *Fawlty Towers*) as little sister Vicky, Jack Howarth (Albert Tatlock from *Coronation Street*) as Tubby and John Laurie (*Dad's Army's* Fraser) as the brusque Scots doctor. *Hobson's Choice* is a delightful film and is a credit to David Lean and his cast. It showcases the charms of old North-West England. The best scenes include the moon in puddles, Will's "it's Oldfield Road for us" and Maggie's "well, you'd better kiss me then". And never has a man gone to his doom with more feeling than John Mills' Will on his wedding night. The film won the Golden Bear at the 4th Berlin International Film Festival and the British Film Academy Award for best British Film in 1954.

Overview

Fewer than three million British homes owned a TV set at the beginning of 1954. These were mainly in London, Manchester, Birmingham, Cardiff and Glasgow. However, those who owned a TV were still very much in the minority. Radio still provided news and entertainment for the majority of the nation. Some programmes such as *Workers' Playtime*, which began during WW2, were still running from 'a factory somewhere in England'. A few performers of that time would turn up at a factory canteen and perform live to the workers. Singers were accompanied by piano only and would perform in between comedy acts by the likes of Arthur Askey, Tommy Trinder and Ted Ray. All were masters of their craft. Morning Radio was heavily slanted towards wives and mothers as

Tommy Trinder (with Jean Colin)

career women were almost unheard of. Programmes included *Housewives' Choice, Music While You Work* and *Mrs. Dale's Diary* (an early soap opera). Afternoon radio was more relaxing and there would be a lunchtime light drama almost every day. Band shows were still thriving at the weekend, with Billy Cotton and Victor Sylvester leading the way. There was also *In Town Tonight* which was a national institution from 1933 to 1960. It was an early form of chat show which included reviews and celebrity gossip, but tame by today's standards. Radio also played a big part in children's lives. At school they could listen to educational programmes such as *Nature Study*. Pre-school children were treated to *Listen with Mother*, which could easily have been titled *Sit Still, Mother Has Something Better To Do*!

Hancock's Half Hour

First aired on radio on the 2nd November 1954
Starring Tony Hancock, Bill Kerr, Moira Lister and Sid James

The series introduced the world to 'the lad himself' namely Anthony Aloysius St. John Hancock, who famously lived at 23 Railway Cuttings, East Cheam. Hancock's situation and career invariably changed depending on the episode, but typically he was portrayed as an out-of-work actor, who had deluded himself that he was more famous than he actually was. He was cantankerous, pompous and comically out of step with the world around him, but most importantly he was endearing so audiences took to him immediately. Building on what *The Goon Show* had achieved in revolutionising radio comedy, *Hancock's Half Hour* was arguably the first series to give a radio comedy true structure and to let the narrative and characters guide the story. This

Moira Lister and Tony Hancock

was the 1950s, where radio was king and television was still just finding its feet; a world almost unimaginable today. The series transferred to television in 1956 where Hattie Jacques, Patricia Hayes and Kenneth Williams joined the cast. The sketch that everyone remembers was the second to last episode ever recorded, *The Blood Donor* (televised in 1961). It is a timeless piece of comedy which, although sixty years old, is as funny now as it was then. The testament to a true comic genius.

Under Milk Wood   First broadcast on The BBC Third Programme on 25th January 1954

"To begin at the beginning: It is spring, moonless night in the small town, starless and bible-black."

Poet and Writer Dylan Thomas

The opening of *Under Milk Wood* draws you into Thomas' story of a day in the life of the inhabitants of the small Welsh seaside village of Llareggub. The very first radio production of Dylan Thomas's *Under Milk Wood* was an immediate success, winning the Prix Italia. It was broadcast on the Third Programme (now Radio 3) on 25th January 1954. This 94-minute version was repeated several times; the Home Service broadcast a shortened version later in the same year. 60-minute versions were made for overseas networks and the play was translated into at least eight languages for radio productions across Europe and beyond. Although it is described as a play in the subtitle, its many characters contribute to no plot or story. It is both a poetic and a documentary piece which describes, through a rich tapestry of narration, dialogue, soliloquy and song, the secrets, longings and regrets of many inhabitants of a fictional Welsh seaside town over the course of a single day. Moments of humour, delight, surprise and pathos come and go fleetingly, yet the 'ear-catching' inventiveness of Dylan Thomas' language means that characterisation is nevertheless readily established, resulting in a richly layered work. The play is saturated with the warts-and-all realities and peculiarities of human experience, but it is curious rather than contemptuous, and generously accepting of the many and varied paths a human life can take. The formal device of narration providing not only structure but also the interpretative key and emotional register for the work. The widely acknowledged triumph of *Under Milk Wood* on radio is closely related to Thomas' linguistic dexterity, poetic sensibility and imaginative flights of fancy. In the 1954 production, Richard Burton opens the play in the role of First Voice, one of the narrator figures. He describes the town of Llareggub, which is said to be situated on the "sloeblack, slow, black, / crowblack, fishingboat-

Richard Burton played First Voice

bobbing sea". "Hush" he says, "for it is night-time and the inhabitants are asleep." Invocations to the listener continue: "You" and "come closer now", and he repeatedly encourages listeners to both "Listen" and "Look'" or, in other words, to pay attention and open their imaginations. "Only you can hear the houses sleeping in the streets in the slow deep salt and silent black, bandaged night. Only you can see, in the blinded bedrooms, the combs. and petticoats over the chairs, the jugs and basins, the glasses of teeth, Thou Shalt Not on the wall, and the yellowing dickybird-watching pictures of the dead. Only you can hear and see, behind the eyes of the sleepers, the movements and countries and mazes and colours and dismays and rainbows and tunes and wishes and flight and fall and despairs and big seas of their dreams." Critics in the press were bowled over. "No more imaginative, more skilfully worked-out design for a radio feature can easily be conceived", declared *The Times* critic.

Lassie

Ran from 12th September 1954 to 24th March 1973
Starring Tommy Rettig, Jan Clayton and George Cleveland

Lassie first touched the hearts of moviegoers in 1943's feature film *Lassie Come Home*, but the talented collie soon switched media, first with a radio series from 1947 to 1950, then with a wildly successful long-running live-action TV series. *Lassie* first lived on a family farm near the town of Calverton, where she was the loving companion of Jeff Miller (Tommy Rettig), his widowed mother, and "Gramps". For three years, Jeff and *Lassie* would rescue each other and anyone else in a perilous situation, always at precisely the right moment. But, when Rettig grew up, the show's producers decided he would 'go off to college' so that they could replace him with a younger actor. Family #2 featured the Martins, who took *Lassie* into their home. The Martins had recently adopted a young orphan named Timmy (Jon Provost), who quickly became *Lassie's* new best pal. But Timmy also grew up, and *Lassie* moved on yet again. This time, the Martins 'moved to Australia'. They left Lassie with old friend, Cully Wilson (Andy Clyde), but when Wilson became sick and *Lassie* ran to forest ranger Corey Stewart (Robert Bray) for help, Wilson decided that the trustworthy ranger could better care for the dog. When Stewart was injured while fighting a fire, he gave *Lassie* to two other rangers, Scott Turner (Jed Allan) and Bob Erickson (Jack de Mave). *Lassie's* new freedom in the forest had given her more confidence, and beginning in 1970, *Lassie* had no single owner and went 'rogue' wandering the town in search of humans in distress.

Zoo Quest

Ran from 21st December 1954 to 31st May 1963
Presented by David Attenborough

The celebrated television naturalist David Attenborough first appeared on our screens in *Zoo Quest*. He went as a producer to Sierra Leone with zoologists Jack Lester and Alfred Woods to film them collecting animals for London Zoo. The footage shot in the wild by cameraman Charles Lagus was augmented in the finished programme with studio sections, where some of the creatures collected were seen up close. When Lester fell ill, Attenborough stepped in as presenter. In a time before mass tourism the places and animals filmed in *Zoo Quest* were unfamiliar to the majority of the audience and had not been seen on television before. In the second series, they went to Borneo in search of the komodo dragon resulting in more unique footage. Attenborough continued presenting throughout the decade, whilst still producing. He went on to become Controller of BBC2 and oversee the introduction of colour television in 1967. Eventually in 1979, he realised his ambition to make a large scale natural history programme using the latest technology with the landmark 13-part series *Life on Earth*. Now, instead of describing the animals as he had to in *Zoo Quest*, he was able to let the colour pictures speak for themselves. In 2016, a researcher looking through the *Zoo Quest* (1954) archives held at the BBC's Natural History Unit in Bristol unearthed more than six hours' worth of original location-shot material on colour 16mm film. (This had been believed to provide better definition on the monochrome 405-line picture of 1950s UK television.) It is available to watch on BBC iPlayer.

1984

Written by George Orwell and adapted for television by Nigel Kneale
Starring Peter Cushing, Yvonne Mitchell and Andre Morrell

George Orwell's novel *1984* was brought to television on 12th December 1954, adapted by Nigel Kneale and directed by Rudolph Cartier. Its vision of a future authoritarian state shocked viewers, particularly the scenes where the hero Winston Smith was tortured in the infamous Room 101. Some MPs and members of the press complained and Cartier received death threats, but the controversy helped popularise the play. When it was repeated days later, it drew the largest audience since the Queen's Coronation of the previous year. *1984* was broadcast live, as was usual at the time, so the repeat was a new performance. Cartier helped the pace of the drama by using pre-cut scenes inserted into the action, making time for more complicated changes between the live sections. Winston Smith was played by Peter Cushing with Yvonne Mitchell as his lover Julia. Andre Morrell was intimidating as Smith's tormentor O'Brien. When *1984* was revised and revived by Kneale in 1965, both television drama and viewers had become more sophisticated, helped in no small part by the trailblazing 1954 original. The later broadcast passed without controversy. Kneale and Cartier continued to work together at the BBC, producing celebrated TV dramas including *Quatermass II*, *Quatermass and the Pit* and *Wuthering Heights*.

Running Wild

First aired on 21st April 1954
Featuring the television debut of Eric Morecambe and Ernie Wise

The duo would become Britain's best loved double act. They had cut their teeth on the northern comedy circuit with their first performance as a duo at the Liverpool Empire in August 1941. After World War 2, they toured the country as part of a variety circus. As their fame grew, they appeared on radio on shows including *Variety Fanfare*. This led to their own radio show in 1953 called *You're Only Young Once*. In 1954, *Running Wild* was to be their big break into television. It was a mixture of music and comedy, the sort of thing America had done successfully for years. The series ran for six episodes and was an abject failure almost finishing the duo's careers before they had really started. They and *Running Wild* received many highly critical and derogatory reviews in newspapers, one of which said "Definition of Television: the box they buried Morecambe and Wise in". Eric carried a cutting of that review in his wallet for the rest of his life. One of the main reasons for their lacklustre performance was that the BBC strongly advised them use BBC scriptwriters and to tone down their northern humour, instead of using their own material which they were more confident about. It was a mistake that Morecambe and Wise would not make again. Eric and Ernie went on to produce some of the most watched shows in British television history with their Christmas Specials becoming as much a part of Yuletide as The Queen's Speech and leftover turkey. In 1977, an estimated 26 million viewers tuned in to watch them.

Nat King Cole

Smile

Sung by Nat King Cole   Written by Chaplin, Turner and Parsons

Peaked at #3 in the UK charts on 16th September 1954

Although he is remembered today principally as a comedian, the multi-disciplined Charlie Chaplin was also a composer. He wrote *Smile* as an instrumental for the 1936 production *Modern Times*, his final silent film. The lyrics were added later by John Turner and Geoffrey Parsons and, like the music, match the tone of the film. Cole's smooth voice was a perfect match for the sentiment of the song "Smile though your heart is aching, smile even though it's breaking." It has been recorded numerous times including by Tony Bennett (1959) and again in a duet with Barbra Streisand (2006), Lady Gaga and Judy Garland. It was also performed at the funeral of Michael Jackson. Michael Bublé recorded a special version for the funeral of Captain Tom Moore, the centenarian charity fundraiser who walked 100 laps of his garden during the COVID-19 pandemic.

Dean Martin

That's Amore

Sung by Dean Martin   Written by Harry Warren and Jack Brooks

Peaked at #2 in the UK charts on 25th February 1954

One of Dean Martin's most famous songs, *That's Amore*, describes love the way they do it in Napoli ("Amore" is Italian for "Love"). Filled with passion, the singer compares the feeling to his favourite Italian foods: pizza and pasta fagiole. It's a quirky romantic song poking a bit of fun at Italian stereotypes, something Martin, born Dino Crocetti, had every right to do. The song first appeared in the 1953 movie *The Caddy*, starring Martin and his comedy partner Jerry Lewis. In his autobiography, Lewis said that when he and Dean were making *The Caddy*, the writers left Dean with little to do. Jerry went behind Dean's back and asked songwriter Harry Warren to write a hit song for Dean to sing in the movie. *That's Amore* was the result. The song has also featured in the films *Rear Window* (1954), *Moonstruck* (1987) and *Bridget Jones's Baby* (2016) among others.

Frank Sinatra

Three Coins in the Fountain

Sung by Frank Sinatra   Written by Jule Styne and Sammy Cahn

#1 in the UK charts for 3 weeks from September 17th 1954

The song was written for a romantic film of the same name and refers to the act of throwing a coin into the Trevi Fountain in Rome while making a wish. Each of the film's three stars performs this act. Cahn and Styne were asked to write the song to fit the movie, but were unable to either see the film or read the script. They completed the song in an hour and had produced a demonstration record with Frank Sinatra by the following day. The song was subsequently used as the film's soundtrack, but in the rush 20th Century Fox neglected to sign a contract with the composers, allowing them to claim complete rights over the royalties. The composers used this to their advantage with a version by Dinah Shore also being released in 1954. The song won the Best Original Song Oscar in 1955.

Rosemary Clooney

This Ole House

Sung by Rosemary Clooney   **Written by Stuart Hamblen**
Released on 25th March 1954

The song was inspired by a dilapidated house that lyricist Hamblen stumbled across on a hunting trip. It imagines the fall into disrepair of what was once a lively family home. It begins telling us that "This old house once rang with laughter" but ends listing undone repair jobs and finally tells us that the house and its owner "are tuckered out" and "a-gettin' ready to meet the saints." Clooney's version reached #1 in both the UK and Billboard charts. It was revived by Welsh rocker Shakin' Stevens in 1981, when it also topped the charts in the UK. It has been covered many times over the decades by such artists as Bette Midler and Brian Setzer. It was used in the soundtrack of the film *Chicken Run* (2000). And if the name Clooney sounds familiar, she was George's aunt.

Doris Day

Secret Love

Sung by Doris Day   **Written by Sammy Fain and Paul Francis Webster**
Winner of the 1954 Academy Award for Best Original Songwriter

Secret Love was composed for *Calamity Jane*, a 1953 musical film in which Doris Day played the title role. The haunting melody bears more than a passing resemblance to the opening theme of Schubert's *A-major piano sonata*. The song reached #1 on both sides of the Atlantic and was in the top 10 best selling songs of 1954. When Day first heard the song, she was so moved by it that she "just about fell apart." The song was so personal to her that Day declined to perform the nominated (and ultimately victorious) *Secret Love* at the Oscars ceremony, later stating: "When they asked me to sing *Secret Love* on Academy Awards night I told them I couldn't, not in front of those people." In 1963, the song would take on a new life in the UK when Kathy Kirby made it her signature tune.

Vera Lynn

My Son, My Son

Sung by Vera Lynn

Written by Gordon Melville, Bob Howard and Eddie Calvert

There were two main reasons that the 'Forces' Sweetheart' Vera Lynn had to wait until 1954 to taste chart-topping success in the UK. First, when she was at the height of her popularity, no records were being pressed as vinyl was needed for the war effort. Secondly, there were no charts measuring record sales in Britain until 1952. It was Lynn's only number one hit, reached towards the end of the peak of her career. Earlier, in 1951, she had reached #1 in the US Billboard chart with her recording of *Auf Wiederseh'n Sweetheart*. *My Son, My Son* was Lynn's fifth chart hit in the UK, following on from *Auf Wiederseh'n Sweetheart*, *Forget-Me-Not*, *The Homing Waltz* (all 1952) and *The Windsor Waltz* (1953). She again tasted chart success some 63 years later when the album *Vera Lynn 100* was released to commemorate her 100th birthday. It peaked at #3 in the UK charts.

Let's Have Another Party

Winifred Atwell

Performed by Winifred Atwell

Reached #1 in the UK charts on 4th December 1954

The medley of tunes played by Trinidad-born pianist Atwell was a follow up to her 1953 hit *Let's Have a Party*. It featured instrumental versions of songs from before the war. As the track progresses a (probably unintended) cautionary tale emerges. It kicks off with *Another Little Drink Wouldn't Do Us Any Harm* and in the middle we hear *I Wonder Where My Baby is Tonight?* A little while later it moves on to *Somebody Stole My Gal*. Maybe that little drink wasn't the best idea. The party ends with *When the Red, Red Robin (Comes Bob, Bob, Bobbin' Along)*. As if to highlight her range Atwell had another hit in 1954, this time with the more cerebral Rachmaninoff's *18th Variation on a Theme by Paganini (The Story of Three Lovers)*, which reached #9 in the charts. Atwell was the first black person to top the charts in the UK.

Rock Around the Clock

Bill Haley

Performed by Bill Haley and his Comets   **Written by Freedman and Myers**

Released as the B-side to Thirteen Women on 20th May 1954

The song was written in 1952, but contractual wrangling meant that Bill Haley could not record it until 1954. It eventually reached #1 in both the United States and United Kingdom charts and also re-entered the UK Singles Chart in the 1960s and 1970s. It was not the first rock and roll record, nor was it the first successful record of the genre. Bill Haley had American chart success with *Crazy Man, Crazy* in 1953 and in 1954, *Shake, Rattle and Roll* sung by Big Joe Turner reached #1 on the Billboard R&B chart. Haley's recording nevertheless became an anthem for rebellious 1950s youth and is widely considered to be the song that, more than any other, brought rock and roll into mainstream culture around the world. The song is ranked No. 158 on the Rolling Stone magazine's list of The 500 Greatest Songs of All Time.

Space Guitar

'Guitar' Watson

Written and Performed by Johnny 'Guitar' Watson

Released in April 1954

When 19-year-old Watson picked up his electric guitar and laid down *Space Guitar* in Los Angeles in February 1954, he would change the world of music forever but few knew it at the time. Although the use of horn music at the beginning of the track placed it firmly in the 1950s, Watson's use of feedback and shredding (fast tempo playing) was at least a decade ahead of its time. Because the track was so difficult to categorise, it went under the radar for many years. However, it is seen as a forerunner to a genre of music embraced by Jimi Hendrix, Frank Zappa and Joe Santana. Watson was also a flamboyant performer and played the guitar with his teeth, behind his head, and while roaming through the audience and beyond .... does that remind you of anyone?

Top of the Pops in 1954

There were 12 number one records in 1954 in the UK single charts published by the NME. The best selling single of the year was *Secret Love* by Doris Day.

	Weeks at number one
Answer Me / Frankie Laine From 1st January 1954 for 1 week	▌
Oh Mein Papa / Eddie Calvert From 8th January 1954 for 9 weeks	▌▌▌▌▌▌▌▌▌
I See The Moon / The Stargazers From 12th March 1954 for 5 weeks then from 23rd April 1954 for 1 week	▌▌▌▌▌▌
Secret Love / Doris Day From 16th April 1954 for 1 week then from 7th May 1954 for 8 weeks	▌▌▌▌▌▌▌▌▌
Such A Night / Johnnie Ray From 30th April 1954 for 1 week	▌
Cara Mia / David Whitfield & Mantovani and his Orchestra From 2nd July 1954 for 10 weeks	▌▌▌▌▌ ▌▌▌▌▌
Little Things Mean A Lot / Kitty Kallen From 10th September 1954 for 1 week	▌
Three Coins In The Fountain / Frank Sinatra From 17th September 1954 for 3 weeks	▌▌▌
Hold My Hand / Don Cornell From 8th October 1954 for 4 weeks then from 19th November for 1 week	▌▌▌▌▌
My Son, My Son / Vera Lynn From 5th November 1954 for 3 weeks	▌▌▌
This Ole House / Rosemary Clooney From 26th November 1954 for 1 week	▌
Let's Have Another Party / Winifred Atwell From 3rd December 1954 for 5 weeks	▌▌▌▌▌

Nine Lessons and Carols from King's College Chapel

King's College Chapel in winter

The Choir of King's College Cambridge was created by Henry VI, who founded King's College in 1441. Its main function was to provide daily singing in his chapel. It is a tradition that remains to this day. Henry VI specified that the choristers were to be poor boys, of strong constitution and of "honest conversation". They had to be under twelve years of age when admitted, and able to read and sing. In addition to their choral duties singing daily Matins, Mass and Vespers, they were to wait at table in Hall. The boys were provided with meals and clothing, and eight pence a week for their board. They were not allowed to wander beyond the college grounds without permission from their Master or the Provost.

Until the late nineteenth century, Christmas carols had only been performed by carol singers visiting people's houses. However, troubled by his parishioner's excessive consumption of alcohol on Christmas Eve, the Right Rev. Edward White Benson (The Bishop of Truro) created a religious celebration of Christmas to tempt revellers into church and out of the pubs. As a result, the first service of nine lessons and carols was held in Truro Cathedral at 10pm on Christmas Eve, 1880. Bishop Benson went on to become the Archbishop of Canterbury and his service started to gain popularity around the nation. In 1918, the new dean of King's College Cambridge, the Rev. Eric Milner-White, oversaw the first Festival of Nine Lessons and Carols at the college. Its fame grew after the service was heard on BBC radio in 1928 and, with the exception of 1930, it has been broadcast at home and abroad ever since. In 1954, Christmas Carols from King's was televised on Christmas Day as part of a live exchange of programmes with other countries, with Midnight Mass coming from Paris on Christmas Eve and Winter Games from Switzerland on Boxing Day. This led to the formation of Eurovision making the event a milestone in broadcasting history. A digitally remastered version of the first Carols from King's College chapel in 1954 gives today's audience a glimpse into the origins of this Christmas tradition. In 2008, the 1954 recording was placed into the National Recording Registry at the US Library of Congress. Today, the service is broadcast live on the BBC World Service and BBC Radio 4.

The Royal Variety Performance on 1st November 1954 at The London Palladium

in the presence of Her Majesty Queen Elizabeth II and His Royal Highness the Duke of Edinburgh

For the 25th Royal Variety Performance (the Silver Jubilee Show) one of the all-time show business greats topped the bill at the Palladium, namely Bob Hope. He was one of the fifteen artistes introduced to the Queen after the show. The others included hardly less famous names such as Noël Coward, Norman Wisdom and Max Bygraves. Once again The Crazy Gang warmed up the audience, who had given the Queen a rousing reception. As part of the warm-up, The Crazy Gang sold ice cream and walked in and out of the Royal Box dressed as cleaners; the first time any artiste had used the Royal Box in this way. As one commentator put it: "All this got the usually stuffed-shirted audience loosened up before the Queen, looking radiant in white with a dazzling diamond tiara, entered the Royal box, followed by Princess Margaret and Prince

Bob Hope

Philip." Bob Hope appeared solo and in a sketch with two other big names on the bill, Noël Coward and Jimmy Edwards. But despite his popularity with the Royal Party, he was not without his critics. One said, "His offering was loosely thrown together and might have been far more telling if it had been more compact." Even for performers known for their sophistication and urbanity, the Royal Performance can be hard on the nerves. Jack Buchanan attributed this in part to the well-to-do audience: "You can see them sitting there dressed to the nines, saying: We've paid twenty guineas a head for our seats so amuse us if you can." In the event, the audience and the critics alike were

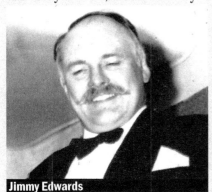
Jimmy Edwards

full of praise for him. *The Times* had this to say on the show: "For charm there was Jack Buchanan aged sixty-three, impersonating a dapper World War One officer and there was no actor on stage with half his sparkle." This year's performance underlined the rich comic talent that was around in Britain at the time with Norman Wisdom, Peter Sellers, Max Bygraves and Frankie Howard all appearing in the show. All four were making their names through the newer mediums of radio and television, but, as *The Stage* commented: "They are already a part of the great tradition of versatile comedy and entertainment and so are often honoured by Royal patronage." Prince Philip exchanged notes with singer Dickie Valentine on the state of married bliss. On asking the whereabouts of Valentine's wife of one week (the ice skater Betty Flynn), the crooner replied that she was in the audience. "What a way to spend a honeymoon," said the Prince.

Norman Wisdom

When the Young British Artists (YBA) burst on the scene in the 1990s, it felt as if they had invented the power to shock through art. However, go back some forty years and Irish born Francis Bacon was producing artwork that still rates as one of the most controversial pieces in the history of art. *Figure with Meat* (1954) portrays Pope Innocent X flanked by two pieces of meat. It is shocking to look at but is open to interpretation. Bacon's pope can be seen alternately as a depraved butcher, or as much a victim as the slaughtered animal hanging behind him. It makes a *Shark in a Tank* (Damien Hirst) or *An Unmade Bed* (Tracey Emin) seem positively mainstream. On a similar iconoclastic theme, surrealist artist Salvador Dali produced his *Crucifixion (Corpus Hypercubus)*. The oil on canvas work sees Christ on a

Salvador Dali

three dimensional cross and can be viewed at the Museum of Modern Art in New York. The most notable classical music production was Benjamin Britten's opera *Turn of the Screw*, based on the 1898 Henry James novella of the same name. It was described by the Guardian as one of the most dramatically appealing of Britten's operas, and by music professor Peter Evans as "Britten's most intricately organised opera." In America, Aaron Copland's only full opera premiered. The composer who is best remembered for *Fanfare for the Common Man*, saw his *The Tender Land* open to universal acclaim at the New York City Opera. It tells of a farm family in the Midwest of the United States. Copland was inspired to write the opera after viewing the Depression-era photographs of Walker Evans. The Nobel Prize in Literature was awarded to the American author Ernest Hemingway "for his mastery of the art of narrative, most recently demonstrated in *The Old Man and the Sea*, and for the influence that he has exerted on contemporary style." The year

Aaron Copland

also saw the publication of two of the greatest works of fiction of the second half of the twentieth century. The first of two J.R.R. Tolkien's *Lord of the Rings* trilogy appeared just months apart. *The Fellowship of the Ring* (July) and *The Two Towers* (Nov) introduced the readers to Middle-earth and would eventually spawn one of the most successful film franchises in history. Another book with lord in the title also appeared this year. *Lord of the Flies* by William Golding, unlike Tolkien's *Lord of the Rings*, described not a battle between good and evil but rather a descent into depravity. In architecture, the Bevin Court Public Housing Project in the London Borough of Finsbury was completed. It provided accommodation for those displaced by The Blitz. Today a one-bedroom flat in the development sells for £500,000. Chief architect Berthold Lubetkin also designed the penguin pool at London Zoo.

J.R.R. Tolkien in his early twenties

The Fellowship of the Ring (Book 1 of The Lord Of The Rings Trilogy)
Author: J.R.R. Tolkien   Published: 29th July 1954

Tolkien wrote *The Hobbit* in 1937. He had fought in and survived one world war but lost some of his best friends. Yet it still seemed possible at that time that one world war might not lead into another. Most of what became the *Lord of the Rings trilogy*, by contrast, was composed during and after the Second World War, It was a time that gave Tolkien plenty of opportunity to contemplate the possible depths of human evil, and to look back at when his own life was touched by the cruelty and horror of war. In his foreword to *The Fellowship of the Ring*, Tolkien writes that "One has indeed personally to come under the shadow of war to feel fully its oppression; but as the years go by it seems now often forgotten that to be caught in youth by 1914 was no less hideous an experience than to be involved in 1939 and the following years. By 1918, all but one of my close friends were dead".

Live and Let Die
Author: Ian Fleming   Published: 5th April 1954

Live and Let Die is the second novel in Ian Fleming's spy thriller series featuring 007, James Bond. The 00 in his code signifies that he is licensed to kill, the 7 means that he is the seventh operative to be given that distinction. The book is grittier than most in the series with the action taking place in Harlem, Florida and Jamaica. The central plot sees Bond trying to catch the truly villainous Mr. Big, a Harlem druglord. It turns out Mr. Big is also Dr. Kananga, a corrupt Jamaican dictator. So on one level he's a sort of Voodoo Baron, but Bond knows he is also an operative for SMERSH who has killed three British agents. He has to put Mr. Big out of business. Fleming drew on his own experiences living in Jamaica for local cultural and geographic references. Although it was met with widespread critical and popular acclaim at the time, its lack of sophistication and racial stereotyping mean that it hasn't travelled as well as other books in the series.

Lucky Jim
Author: Kingsley Amis   Publication Date: January 1954

Amis, who was born in London, wrote poetry, criticism and short stories. He is best remembered as the novelist whose works offered a comic deconstruction of post-war Britain. He explored his disillusionment with British society in the novel *That Uncertain Feeling* (1955). His other works include *The Green Man* (1970) and *The Old Devils* (1986) which won the Booker Prize. In *Lucky Jim*, his first published novel, Jim Dixon has accidentally fallen into a job at one of Britain's leading universities. A moderately successful future in the History Department beckons as long as Jim can stave off the unwelcome advances of fellow lecturer Margaret, survive a madrigal-singing weekend at Professor Welch's and resist Christine, the hopelessly desirable girlfriend of Welch's awful son Bertrand. Inspired by Amis's friend, the poet Philip Larkin, Jim Dixon is a timeless comic character adrift in a hopelessly gauche and pretentious world.

Under The Net

Author: Iris Murdoch   First Published in 1954

Iris Murdoch was born in Dublin in 1919 of Anglo-Irish parents. She went to Badminton School, Bristol and read classics at Somerville College, Oxford. In 1948, she returned to Oxford where she became a fellow of St. Anne's college. She was one of the 20th century's most influential novelists and also a distinguished philosopher. This, her first novel, is set in a part of London where struggling writers rub shoulders with film starlets and shady underworld figures. Its hero, Jake Donaghue, is a drifting, clever, likeable young man, who makes a living out of translation work and sponging off his friends. A meeting with Anna, an old flame, leads him into a series of fantastic adventures. Jake is captivated by a majestic philosopher, Hugo Belfounder, whose profound and inconclusive reflections give the book its title "under the net of language." Robust, full of flavour and panache, it is a rare novel that makes one laugh and think in equal measure.

Destination Unknown

Author: Agatha Christie   First Published: 1st November 1954

The novel represents a change of genre for Christie. A famous British scientist, Thomas Betterton, has gone missing. With conflicting reports of sightings, British intelligence are edgy. Betterton is the inventor of ZE Fusion (a radioactive substance) which malevolent forces who would like to get their hands on. Other scientists have also disappeared. A man called Jessop invites Betterton's wife, Olive, in for a little chat. No one is quite sure if she knows of her husband's whereabouts. Olive Betterton is exhausted from the press speculation and worry and asks permission to go abroad to get away from it all. She chooses Morocco. Permission granted she sets off, a carefully orchestrated tail in close pursuit. However, Olive's plane to Casablanca crashes, and she lies unconscious in hospital, one of just a few survivors. The doctors predict she won't live long. Thereafter the novel has several twists involving impostors, spies and shady characters.

Twelve Angry Men

Author: Reginald Rose   First Published and Performed in 1954

The entire play takes place in the jury room, leaving the audience to piece together the facts of the case from the deliberations. A young man has been charged with first-degree murder, for killing his father. His alibi is weak, and considerable circumstantial evidence links him to the crime. What is more, the death penalty is on the table. The jurors are referred to by number, not by name, which adds to the play's power and intensity. Initially all but one juror votes guilty. Over the course of the play the lone holdout attempts to convince the others there is reasonable doubt, and that they should acquit. It gained wider prominence in 1957 when it was turned into a film directed by Sidney Lumet starring Henry Fonda and Lee J. Cobb. The drama's universal themes have seen productions in England, Russia, Pakistan and Japan. For some theatrical adaptations, where female actors are cast, the play is often re-titled *12 Angry People or 12 Angry Jurors*.

Lord of the Flies

Author: William Golding   Publication Date: 17th September 1954

In the near future an aircraft catches fire, crashes and lands on a deserted isolated South Seas island in the middle of an atomic war. All the grown-ups are killed leaving only a group of children 12 and younger that survive. Ralph is chosen leader, and 'Piggy' becomes his intellectual sidekick. Where they have landed at first seems like paradise. It is a beautiful green tropical coral isle with a blue lagoon and magnificent palm trees. Better still are coconut trees and plenty of other fruit to eat. There is also an abundance of wild pigs in the forest and plenty of fish in the ocean. Soon rivalries in the group abound. The book examines the author's belief in the battle between good and evil contained within the human spirit. The children are confronted by a beast from the mountains. Imagined or not, it further divides them. Later, two tribes emerge and there is a struggle for supremacy on the island....will the wicked inherit the Earth?

The Horse And His Boy

Author: C.S. Lewis   Publication Date: 6th September 1954

The Horse and his Boy is a stirring and dramatic fantasy story that finds a young boy named Shasta on the run from his homeland with the talking horse, Bree. When the pair discover a deadly plot by the Calormen people to conquer the land of Narnia, the race is on to warn the inhabitants of the impending danger and to rescue them all from certain death. To the south of Narnia lies a vast desert, and beyond that the Calormen Empire. Deep within Calormen the bedraggled and misused Thasta, the son of a fisherman, and Aravis, who is due to be forced into a terrible arranged marriage, find themselves unlikely travel companions on the road to the fabled Narnia. This was the fifth book published in the series, but the third chronologically. It features all the elements of the classic children's tale: 'evil' empire, kings, queens, battles, giants, as well as the usual Narnian talking animals.

Horton Hears A Who!

Author: Dr. Seuss   Published: 12th August 1954

The story follows an outgoing elephant named Horton. He lives a cosy life until the day when he hears a noise. What is that noise you may ask? A tiny yelp, and Horton thinks it's coming from a minute creature called a Who. Horton is after all an elephant and elephants have big ears so only Horton can hear the voices coming from a tiny speck! The voices ask Horton to help them find a stable, quiet place where they can exist harmoniously. Horton is very willing to do so but there is a problem. The head kangaroo that runs the jungle Horton lives in doesn't believe in the tiny Who. She doesn't like to believe in anything she can't see, hear or smell. She insists that Horton is crazy and that everyone needs to help get rid of the speck for good! Horton simply cannot put up with that. Thus begins his truly epic journey to save the Who. The book was made into a film in 2008, featuring the voice talents of Jim Carrey and Steve Carell.

Barbara Hepworth & Henry Moore

Barbara Hepworth and Henry Moore were two of the most influential British artists of the 20th century. They were both sculptors who contributed significantly to the development of modern art and the abstract movement. While they shared many similarities in their artistic styles and careers, they also had some notable differences. Barbara Hepworth was born in Wakefield, Yorkshire in 1903, and Henry Moore was born in Castleford, Yorkshire in 1898. Both artists were influenced by the natural landscape of their home region, which can be seen in their works. Hepworth studied at Leeds School of Art and then at the Royal College of Art in London. Moore also studied at the Royal College of Art but his studies were temporarily interrupted by military service during World War I. Both artists were also inspired by the works of Constantin Brancusi and Pablo Picasso, as well as the ancient cultures of Africa and Mexico. Hepworth's early works were figurative, but she gradually moved towards abstraction and began to incorporate elements of the landscape into her sculptures. She became associated with the British abstract movement, which emphasised simplicity, geometry and the use of pure forms. She was one of the few female artists who achieved significant success in this male-dominated field. Her works were often made of materials such as marble, bronze and wood featuring smooth, organic shapes. Moore's early works were also figurative, but he too gradually moved towards abstraction. He is perhaps best known for his large, abstract sculptures of reclining figures. His works were often made of materials such as bronze, stone and wood and featured rough, organic shapes. Moore was also interested in the relationship between the sculpture and its environment, and many of his works were designed to be displayed outdoors. Despite their similarities, Hepworth and Moore had different approaches to sculpture. Hepworth's works were often more intimate and delicate, while Moore's were more monumental and forceful. Hepworth was more interested in the inner qualities of the materials she used, while Moore focused more on the outer shapes they created. Both artists, however, were deeply committed to the idea that sculpture convey emotions and ideas in a way that was different to other forms of art. In 1954, Hepworth produced the wooden carving *Corinthos* after a visit to the Greek city. Moore was prolific in 1954 creating works including the bronze castings of *Reclining Figure: External Form* and *Large Upright Internal/External Form.*

Reclining Figure - Moore

Single Form - Hepworth

Reclining Figure: External Form - Moore

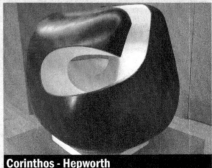
Corinthos - Hepworth

John Masefield, Poet Laureate (served 1930-1967)

John Masefield

Masefield was the longest serving Poet Laureate to serve entirely within the 20th century. His 37 years of service was only beaten by Alfred, Lord Tennyson who held the post between 1850-1892. By the 1950s, Masefield seemed to be from a bygone era as traditional poetry had fallen out of favour as modernist poets such as Sylvia Plath and Stevie Smith were gaining traction. The emerging Beat Generation of poets such as Ginsburg, Carr and Huncke seemed to speak more to the youth of the day than did the rather staid Masefield. Still, he took his job seriously and acted as all good Poets Laureate do. He wrote poems for the court, in his case the House of Windsor. Rather quaintly Masefield would send his poems to The Times of London for their approval with a stamped addressed envelope for their response. Even though he seemed more like a 19th century poet than most of his contemporaries, many of his poems still stand the test of time. His *Sonnets and Poems* written in the midst of World War I and *A Generation Risen* written during World War II defined him as a chronicler of British 20th century history and one of the few poets to have written during both wars. In 1954, Masefield unveiled a mural tablet in Westminster Abbey to the poets Keats and Shelley.

The Role of Poet Laureate Through The Ages

The monarch of the day bestows the honorary position of Poet Laureate, currently on the advice of the prime minister. There are no specific duties to the role although it is expected that the holder produces original verse to commemorate significant national occasions. The first official Poet Laureate was John Dryden who was appointed by Charles II in 1668. Until Andrew Motion was appointed in 1999, the laureateship was held for life; subsequently the position has been offered for a fixed term of 10 years. Other notable Poet Laureates included William Wordsworth (1843-1850), Sir John Betjeman (1972-1984) and Ted Hughes (1984-1998). The actor Daniel Day-Lewis's father, Cecil, was also Poet Laureate from 1968 to 1972. It was only in 2009 that the first woman, Carol Ann Duffy, was offered the role. She was also the first Scot.

Sir John Betjeman

Carol Ann Duffy

The role of Poet Laureate is not a money spinner; Andrew Motion and Carol Ann Duffy were offered annual salaries of £5,750 per year. However, in a quirky tradition dating back to Charles I, the holder also receives a barrel of sherry.

TRADIC

The first TRADIC being assembled

TRADIC or **TRA**nsitor **DI**gital **C**omputer was the world's first transistorised computer built by Bell Labs for the United States Air Force. It took nearly 3 years to build and was completed in January 1954. Prior to TRADIC, early computers used vacuum tubes for memory, signal processing and switching. However, vacuum tubes were bulky, generated a lot of heat and had a short life span. Transistors, which in effect are tiny electrical switches, offered huge benefits by being much smaller, more energy efficient, more reliable, much cheaper and faster. This first TRADIC machine was built to evaluate the feasibility of an airborne computer on board a USAAF B-52 Stratofortress plane to control the bombing and navigation systems. The US military then proposed a second application for the TRADIC on board a warship for a 'track-while-scan' radar system. As with many technological innovations, the initial military application opened the door to the development of smaller and faster computers used by the civilian population. The TRADIC computer of January 1954 paved the way for compact, lightweight and affordable computing that has completely transformed all aspects of our daily lives.

The World's First Commercially Produced Transistor Radio

The Regency TR-1 Transistor Radio

When Texas Instruments was looking for a radio manufacturer to develop a radio using their new transistors, none of the leading radio brands of the day were interested. Instead a producer of home antenna boosters stepped in. This lead to the launch of the Regency TR-1 in November 1954; it was the world's first hand-held consumer radio. Although portable radios using vacuum tubes were available, the use of tiny transistors allowed the design of the TR-1 to be ultra compact for the time; it measured just 3" x 5" x 1¼". It cost $49.95 which is the equivalent of over $500 in today's money. It used a single 22.5 volt rectangular battery which would give it 20-30 hours use which was much longer than the vacuum tube equivalents. The bold styling for the time won an award from the Industrial Design Society of New York. It was also selected by the Museum of Modern Art for an exhibition in Paris in 1955. The red triangles on the dial indicated the frequencies used by the US government for emergency broadcasts in the event of enemy attack during the Cold War. Due to cost cutting in the circuitry to keep the total cost down, the sound quality was not great. As a result only 150,000 units were sold. They are now collectors items.

The Birth of Non-Stick Cookware

AMAZING NEW CONCEPT IN *Cooking*

FREE SPATULA WITH EACH "HAPPY PAN"

NOTHING STICKS TO *"HAPPY PAN"*

A cast iron skillet sealed with DuPont TEFLON®

An early advert for a non-stick pan

In 1954, Marc Grégoire was an engineer at the French national aerospace research centre (ONERA) in the suburbs of Paris. He and his colleague were investigating the use of PTFE (Polytetrafluoroethylene) to coat aluminium moulds used in making fibre glass fishing rods to make their removal easier. PTFE, better known by the DuPont's brand name Teflon, was invented in 1938. When Grégoire's wife, Colette, heard about the experimentation, she challenged her husband to create a non-stick saucepan. He succeeded in coating the base of an aluminium saucepan with Teflon and subsequently successfully patented the invention later that year. This would lead to the couple setting up the Tefal Corporation in 1956. Tefal is a blend of the words **TEF**lon and **AL**uminium. Under the slogan of "The Tefal saucepan, the saucepan that doesn't really stick", the couple would go on to build a hugely successfully company. By 1960, they were selling 3 million non-stick cookware items per year. However, DuPont objected to the use of the name Tefal in the United States as it too closely resembled their trademark 'Teflon'. As a result, Tefal is marketed as T-fal in the US. The T-fal name is also used in Canada and Japan.

The Invention of the Angle Grinder

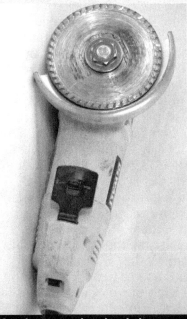

A mains powered angle grinder

One of the most popular handheld power tools was invented in 1954. The introduction of the angle grinder revolutionised the world of metalworking and construction. This versatile power tool, with its distinct handheld design, enabled professionals and DIY enthusiasts to cut, grind, and polish materials with unprecedented ease and precision. It was developed by German manufacturer Ackermann + Schmitt (FLEX-Elektrowerkzeuge GmbH). The company was founded in 1922 to produce flexible shaft grinders. However, their angle grinder invention turbocharged their fortunes. The angle grinder is known by different names around the world including side grinder, disc grinder and even FLEX (after the company name). Ackermann + Schmitt angle grinders were originally electrically powered and featured a rapidly rotating disc with abrasive surfaces, which could grind and cut through metal, stone, and other materials with remarkable efficiency. Over the years new designs and improved safety features including cordless grinders, compressed air power, variable speeds, disc brakes and kickback reduction systems have made the angle grinder one of the most versatile power tools available.

The USS Nautilus

Sharing its name with Captain Nemo's fictional submarine in Jules Verne's *Twenty Thousand Leagues Under the Sea*, the USS Nautilus was the world's first nuclear powered submarine. Admiral Hyman G. Rickover, who became known as the 'Father of the Nuclear Navy' led the top secret project from concept design in 1950 to launch in 1954. Powered by a Submarine Thermal Reactor (a pressurised water reactor), the USS Nautilus had virtually limitless power and endurance. This was a game-changer rendering anti-submarine warfare techniques from World War II virtually useless. She was christened on the 21st January 1954 by Mamie Eisenhower, wife of the president. With a crew of just over 100 sailors, the USS Nautilus could silently cruise underwater for thousands of miles without needing to surface. In 1958, the Nautilus achieved a historic milestone by completing the first submerged transit beneath the North Pole as part of 'Operation Sunshine'. This submarine set the new global standard for design, remaining in service until 1980. She can now be explored by visitors at the Submarine Force Library and Museum in Groton, Connecticut, USA.

The USS Nautilus on sea trials

The World's First Nuclear Power Plant

The Obninsk Nuclear Power Facility

The 'science city' of Obninsk lies just under 70 miles southwest of Moscow in Russia. Based at the Institute of Physics and Power Engineering, APS-1 Obninsk (Atomic Power Station 1 Obninsk) was the world's first grid-connected nuclear power plant. Construction started in 1950. The first stable nuclear chain reaction (criticality) was achieved on the 6th May 1954 with connection to the local power grid completed the following month. The single Atom Mirny (Russian for 'Peaceful Atom') reactor was capable of producing 5 MW of power. This was not large scale production as 5 megawatts could typically power around 1000 houses. In addition to power generation, the Obninsk facility also hosted the world's first nuclear medicine centre. Radioactive isotopes produced at the plant were used for medical treatments and diagnostics. The AM-1 reactor at Obninsk operated for 48 years before decommissioning in 2002. During that time there were no major incidents or accidents demonstrating the feasibility of safe nuclear power generation. The AM-1 reactor was the forerunner to the Soviet Union's much larger graphite-moderated RBMK reactors (including Chernobyl's reactor number 4). Today the Obninsk site is home to a nuclear power plant museum.

The Castle Bravo Thermonuclear Weapon Test

The Castle Bravo mushroom cloud

The island paradise of Bikini Atoll is located in the Marshall Islands in the middle of the Pacific Ocean. After World War II, the US continued its nuclear weapon development program. Bikini Atoll was chosen as a test site due to its distance from major land based populations and international shipping lanes. In total, the US detonated 23 nuclear devices between 1946 and 1958 on land, underwater and in the air. In 1954, as part of Operation Castle, the Bravo test remains the US's most powerful nuclear device ever detonated. The explosion was equivalent to 15 million tonnes of TNT, which is over 1000 times more powerful than the atomic bombs dropped on Hiroshima and Nagasaki. The massive explosion produced an intense fireball and a mushroom cloud that reached heights of 130,000 feet. The fallout from the test spread over a wide area, affecting nearby atolls and leading to radioactive contamination. The test's unintentional consequences included irradiating a Japanese fishing vessel, which drew international condemnation and increased public awareness of the dangers of nuclear testing. The original inhabitants of Bikini Atoll continue to battle for compensation as it is still unsafe to inhabit the island.

The Foundation of CERN

Part of the Large Hadron Collider

The Conseil Européen pour la Recherche Nucléaire better known as CERN was established on the 29th September 1954. The acronym is also used for the name of its laboratory based in Meyrin, Switzerland. The council tasked with developing the Meyrin site was initially based at the University of Copenhagen under the direction of the Nobel prize winning Danish physicist Niels Bohr. CERN's original mission was the study of atomic nuclei, but this soon expanded to the study of interactions between subatomic particles. CERN is best known for its particle accelerators, particularly the Large Hadron Collider (LHC), which came online in 2010. The LHC is the most powerful particle accelerator ever built, allowing scientists to study subatomic particles and the fundamental forces of the universe at energies never before attainable. Its most celebrated achievement came in 2012 with the discovery of the Higgs boson, a particle essential to our understanding of how matter acquires mass. More recently, CERN is investigating dark matter. CERN is also the birthplace of the World Wide Web through a project named ENQUIRE initiated by web founder Sir Tim Berners-Lee in 1989.

The First Successful Human Kidney Transplant

In 1954, 23-year-old Richard Herrick from Massachusetts, USA was dying from chronic kidney disease. Two days before Christmas on the 23rd December he received the most precious present anyone could receive from his identical twin Ronald, the gift of life. Ronald had donated one of his kidneys so that Richard could undergo what would turn out to be the world's first successful kidney transplant. It was performed at the Peter Bent Brigham Hospital in Boston by Dr. Joseph Murray. The operation lasted a gruelling five and half hours. Dr. Murray led a team of noted physicians to assist him including Dr. John Hartwell Harrison who had

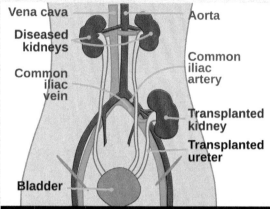

How a transplanted kidney is connected in the body

the task of removing the healthy kidney from Ronald. This was notable for being the first time ever a healthy patient elected for major surgery that was not for his own benefit. Dr. Murray then transplanted Ronald's healthy kidney into Richard's body. The twins had been selected for this groundbreaking surgery due to their genetic similarity which would be a crucial factor in ensuring the transplant's success. Richard was given a new lease of life and lived for a further 8 years. His brother Ronald only died in 2010. Dr. Murray was latterly awarded a Nobel Prize in Physiology or Medicine in 1990 for his groundbreaking work.

The Largest Medical Experiment in History

Thomas Francis Jr.

The poliovirus was first isolated in 1909. In humans it causes poliomyelitis, commonly shortened to polio, which is an infectious disease that is highly transmissible. Around 75% of cases are asymptomatic, but a small percentage of cases can lead to serious symptoms including paralysis, and possible death in extreme cases. In the 1930s, polio spread fear amongst the public as little was know about how to prevent it or stop transmission. Virologists raced to develop a vaccine. In the US, Maurice Brodie and Joseph Kolmer both produced early vaccines but these failed to take hold due to safety concerns from early trials. It wasn't until 1952 that the first effective vaccine was developed by Jonas Salk at the University of Pittsburgh. However, given the failures of previous attempts, the largest medical experiment in history to date was conducted in 1954. It was known as the Francis Field Trial, as it was led by Dr. Thomas Francis Jr. He was an eminent virologist who was the first to isolate influenza in the US in the late 1930s; he was also Salk's tutor and mentor whilst Salk was a student. The field trial involved 1.8 million children across 44 states. Around 440,000 were given doses of the Salk vaccine, 210,000 were given a placebo whilst 1.2 million were observed as a control group to see if any contracted polio. The results of the study were published on 12th April 1955 and showed that the Salk vaccine was 60-70% effective against Type 1 polio and 90% effective against Types 2 and 3. A mass immunisation campaign followed. In 1953, there were 35,000 cases of polio in the US. By 1961, this figure had dropped to only 161 cases.

Linus Carl Pauling

Linus Pauling with his Nobel prize

Linus Carl Pauling was listed by popular science magazine, *New Scientist*, as one of the 20 greatest scientists of all time. He was born in California at the beginning of the 20th century. His CV is remarkable: chemist, chemical engineer, biochemist, peace activist, author, and educator. He was one of the founders in the fields of molecular biology and quantum chemistry. In particular, his work on the theory of chemical bonds led to him being awarded the 1954 Nobel Prize in Chemistry. His discoveries inspired Watson, Crick, Franklin and Wilkins in deciphering the structure of DNA. He also pioneered molecular genetics when discovering that people with sickle cell anaemia had their disease caused by an abnormal protein at molecular level. Although Pauling had been active in supporting the war effort with research and innovation, his views would change radically following the shocking aftermath of the Manhattan Project and the bombs dropped on Hiroshima and Nagasaki. He joined other leading scientists from 1946 onwards including Albert Einstein in warning of the dangers of nuclear proliferation. His ceaseless peace campaigning earned him the Nobel Peace Prize in 1962. He is only one of two people to win Nobel prizes in different fields, the other being Marie Curie. However, he is the only person ever to win two unshared Nobel prizes.

Max Born

Max Born

Max Born was born in 1882 in Poland to a family of Jewish descent. His father was the Professor of Embryology at the local university so Max's path into science was almost assured. However, he didn't just become a scientist, he became a scientific luminary whose life was studded with extraordinary achievements. His exceptional talents were spotted whilst studying at university in Göttingen, Germany. With the rise of the Nazi party in 1933, Born looked to emigrate as his job at the University of Göttingen was at first suspended, then terminated in 1935. He accepted a role at the University of Edinburgh where he continued his work and became a naturalised British citizen one day before war broke out in Europe in 1939. His revolutionary interpretation of quantum mechanics led him to becoming an integral part of the scientific renaissance of the early 20th century alongside Albert Einstein and Erwin Schrödinger. He introduced wave functions as a cornerstone of quantum physics, fundamentally altering our understanding of atomic and subatomic worlds. Born was awarded the 1954 Nobel Prize in Physics alongside his colleague, Werner Heisenberg. The same year he retired from his work, aged 72, and moved back to Germany. An interesting footnote is that Born's daughter, Irene, had married an MI5 officer named Brinley Newton-John who worked on the Enigma project at Bletchley Park during World War II. Their daughter, born in Cambridge in 1948, was singer and actress Olivia Newton-John.

Alan Turing: Genius and War Hero

Alan Mathison Turing was an English mathematician, computer scientist, logician, cryptanalyst, philosopher and theoretical biologist. Born in Maida Vale, London, Turing was raised in southern England. He graduated from King's College, Cambridge with a degree in mathematics. Turing was highly influential in the development of theoretical computer science, providing a formalisation of the concepts of algorithm and computation with the Turing machine, which can be considered a model of a general-purpose computer. He is widely considered to be the father of theoretical computer science and artificial intelligence. Turing has an extensive legacy including statues and many things named after him, for example an annual award for computer science innovations. A 2019 BBC series, as voted by the audience, named him the greatest person of the 20th century. It is estimated that Turing's work breaking Nazi codes during WWII shortened the war by two years and thus saved over 14 million lives. Cracking the code was a silent victory for the war hero who never wore a military

Alan Turing pictured in 1936

uniform. Clearly the hard work, shrouded in secrecy at Bletchley Park, was not done for honour and glory but simply out of duty for the greater good of mankind. After the war, he worked on developing some of the earliest computer programs. Turing was gay, which was illegal in Britain at the time. In 1952, while working at Manchester University, where he had a relationship with a technician called Arnold Murray, he was arrested and charged with gross indecency. He escaped prison only by agreeing to chemical castration through doses of oestrogen which curator David Rooney said had a devastating effect on him both mentally and physically. In 1954 he was found dead in his bed, a half eaten apple on the table beside him, probably laced with the cyanide which killed him. The apple was never tested. It is a national disgrace that a man who saved so many lives through his genius could not be left to live his own life how he wanted. That he now appears on the current Bank of England £50 note, which was released on 23rd June 2021, is scant reward for a man of his greatness. The note features a photo of Turing taken in 1951 by Elliott and Fry which is in the National Portrait Gallery's collection and a table and mathematical formulae from Turing's 1936 paper "On Computable Numbers, with an application to the Entscheidungsproblem"-foundational for computer science.

ALAN TURING
1912 - 1954
Founder of computer science and cryptographer, whose work was key to breaking the wartime Enigma codes, lived and died here.

Blue plaque outside Alan Turing's former home in Wilmslow, Cheshire

It also features the Automatic Computing Engine (ACE) Pilot Machine (the trial model of Turing's design and one of the first electronic stored-program digital computers), technical drawings for the British Bombe (the machine specified by Turing and one of the primary tools used to break Enigma-enciphered messages) and poignantly ticker tape depicting Alan Turing's birth date (23rd June 1912) in binary code. The concept of a machine fed by binary tape featured in Turing's 1936 paper.

The Journey to Elvis Presley's First Record

Elvis Aaron Presley was born on the 8th January 1935 in a two-room 'shotgun' house built by his father in Tupelo, Mississippi. Tragically, his identical twin Jesse Garon Presley was stillborn. Elvis faced humble beginnings with Presley's father, Vernon, struggling to provide for the young family. Vernon was jailed in 1938 for altering a cheque leading to the Presley's losing their house. This forced Elvis and his mother, Gladys, to move in with relatives. Although Elvis was an average student at school, his singing voice was spotted at a young age. Encouraged by a

Elvis Presley's birthplace

teacher to enter, he first sang in public aged 10 in a singing contest at the Mississippi–Alabama Fair and Dairy Show; he came fifth. A few months later on his 11th birthday, Elvis received his first guitar. Apparently he had been hoping for a bicycle or rifle, so his trajectory into music at this age was not a calling. During his teenage years, Elvis slowly learnt how to play the guitar and became a devotee of a radio show hosted by hillbilly singer, Mississippi Slim. At school he was often bullied, seen as a shy loner. This all changed in 1953, when aged 18 in his senior year and with growing confidence, he entered in the school's annual 'Minstrel' show. He sang and played the guitar to a recent hit, *Till I Waltz Again with You*. He is quoted

A publicity shot from 1954

as saying "I wasn't popular in school ... I failed music—only thing I ever failed. And then they entered me in this talent show ... when I came onstage I heard people kind of rumbling and whispering and so forth, 'cause nobody knew I even sang. It was amazing how popular I became after that." Later in 1953, having finished school, Presley tried to make an impression in the music industry by paying to record a couple of songs at a local recording studio, but nothing really came of it. In January 1954, he was turned down at an audition for a vocal group, later telling his father: "They told me I couldn't sing." By Spring 1954, he had taken a job as a truck driver. At this time, his friend who had played a couple of local gigs with, recommended he audition for the Eddie Bond band. Bond, a rockabilly singer, also rejected Presley telling him to stick to truck driving "because you're never going to make it as a singer." However, Elvis's run of rejections and disappointment was about to change. Sam Phillips, the owner of the recording studio where Elvis had recorded his first two songs, was always on the lookout for the next big thing. He'd spotted something in Elvis and was keen to try him out with a couple of local musicians in a recording session. On the evening of 5th July 1954, Elvis, guitarist Winfield 'Scotty' Moore and upright bass player Bill Black tried, without success, to impress Phillips. Just as they were packing up to go home, Elvis started jumping around and singing a 1946 blues number by Arthur Crudup titled *That's Alright*. Black picked up his bass and started jumping around too. After Moore joined in as well, Phillips jumped out of the control booth and asked what they were doing. They said they were just messing around. Phillips asked them to back up and he started recording. Three days later the well known Memphis disc jockey, Dewey Phillips, played the track on his show. There was such an instant reaction from listeners that he then played the track on repeat for the next two hours. A single was then pressed and the rest, as they say, is history!

The First Ascent of K2

The 1950s was a golden age of mountaineering. By 1950, only the tenth highest mountain of the ten highest, Annapurna 1, had been climbed. Within the next ten years all ten had been conquered. The most famous climb was made by the Everest expedition of 1953 where Edmund Hillary invited local, Tensing Norgay, to stand on the peak first. There was no such chivalry in 1954 when a team of Italians nearly came to blows as they climbed the second highest peak K2, nicknamed 'The Killer'. There was never any debate

The summit of K2 stands at 8,611 metres

over whether Achille Compagnoni and Lino Lacedelli summitted the mountain, photographic evidence put that beyond doubt. However, there was controversy for decades over how Hunza porter Amir Mehdi and young climber Walter Bonatti ended up having to bivouac out in the open, without a tent or even a sleeping bag, at an altitude of 8100m. It was

Lino Lacedelli

in 1954, one year on from Hillary and Tensing's ascent of Mount Everest, that an Italian expedition led by Ardito Desio set out to climb K2. The team reached base camp on 28th May. There were 11 Italian climbers, amongst them Compagnoni, Lacedelli and Bonatti, the youngest climber. There were also 10 Hunza high-altitude porters, the equivalent of the Sherpas in Nepal. Desio was a divisive leader. Reports suggest he chose not to bring Riccardo Cassin, a leading Italian Alpinist, because it would have shifted the spotlight off himself. Behind his back the climbers called him "il Ducetto"-Little Mussolini. Desio would issue written orders and motivational messages for climbers. One read: "Remember if you succeed in scaling the peak, as I am confident you will, the entire world will hail you as champions of your race and your fame will endure throughout your lives and long after you're dead. Thus even if you never achieve anything else of note, you will be able to say that you have not lived in vain." Lacedelli is quoted as saying: "We just ignored him and got on with it". By 28th July, Bonatti, Lacedelli and Compagnoni had established Camp VIII, at the altitude of 7627m. Compagnoni and Lacedelli attempted to climb higher and establish the final camp before the summit, the now infamous Camp IX, but couldn't find a suitable location so they returned to Camp VIII. They also realised that they would need supplemental oxygen for the summit push. It was agreed the next day that Compagnoni and Lacedelli would go ahead and establish Camp IX. Bonatti would descend to just above Camp VII to get the supplementary oxygen tanks and then climb back up the mountain to Camp IX, the more challenging of the two tasks given it meant descending 180m then re-ascending 490m back up the mountain carrying oxygen sets weighing 18kg each. Compagnoni wanted to spend the night on the summit, but Lacedelli wanted to head back down immediately. He got his way only after threatening Compagnoni with his ice axe. The summit of K2 was not reached again until 1977.

Compagnoni on K2's summit

The Blons Avalanche

In January 1954, devastating avalanches swept across Austria's Vorarlberg state. In a 48-hour period 388 avalanches were observed. The aftermath was disastrous: 270 burials resulting in 125 deaths, 55 houses and hundreds of farm buildings destroyed, and 500 cattle killed. The Grosswalsertal valley and the village of Blons were the hardest hit. Ultimately, the avalanche cycle led to improved knowledge, practices and tools in avalanche dynamics, the construction of stronger defence structures and more focused avalanche forecasting. After

Blons is surrounded by 6,500ft peaks

an exceptionally warm and dry autumn, the first real snows did not fall until just before Christmas and were followed by two weeks of cold, dry weather. By the second week of January high pressure had formed over the Bay of Biscay and low pressure over Scandinavia. The combination resulted in a strong and moist north-westerly flow that swept into Austria's Northern Alps on January 9th. By January 11th, up to 2 metres of snow had fallen across

The terrifying power of an avalanche

Vorarlberg, and heavy snow continued to fall. As the storm continued to rage, temperatures had also started to warm. Heavy, warmer snow fell onto cold, light snow. On Monday morning the Avalanche Warning System's bulletin, read over local radio warned, "The danger of avalanches has become extremely serious and is still increasing." High above Blons the widely-spaced trees, dilapidated snow fences and walls were no match for the deep, fresh snows. A huge avalanche released from the Flavkopf and slammed into the east side of the village at 10:00. Eighty-two residents were buried, most in houses or barns, and 34 died. A small avalanche late that afternoon killed another person, and at 21:00 a second monstrous avalanche fell from Mont Calv and hit the village centre. Forty-three people were buried, including 16 who had been buried in the morning's avalanche, and another 22 died. The storm had knocked out power and telephone services even before the first avalanche struck. Word of the village's plight did not reach rescuers until a day later. The first rescuers did not reach Blons until January 13th and an international rescue effort soon followed. Rescuers from Germany, Switzerland and the United States soon joined Austrian rescuers. The US Air Force flew 99 helicopter flights to Blons transporting rescuers, evacuating injured patients, as well as dropping off 11,000kg of relief supplies. The Swiss Air-Rescue dispatched 14 rescuers, 6 dog teams and 2 helicopters, as well as a DC-3 with 5 rescue paratroopers and 2 doctors. About half of the buried victims in Blons survived and most were found quickly, however some were buried for many hours. The last survivor was freed after 62 hours. Post-mortem studies of those killed found: "Only a few of the victims died at the moment they were struck by the avalanche."

Rescuers and soldiers pictured during the aftermath

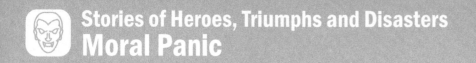
A Vampire is Spotted in Glasgow

Glasgow's Southern Necropolis Gatehouse

On 23rd September 1954, children aged between 4 and 14 years armed themselves with knives and stakes and marched on Glasgow's sprawling Southern Necropolis graveyard. They had heard that two children had been eaten alive at the place known locally as 'The City of the Dead', where 250,000 bodies were buried. The only suspect was a 7ft tall, iron-toothed vampire. Ronnie Sanderson who was aged 8 at the time recounted the tale: "It all started in the playground. The word was there was a vampire and everyone was going to head out there after school. At three o'clock the school emptied and everyone made a beeline for it. We sat there for ages on the wall waiting and waiting. I wouldn't go in because it was a bit scary for me. I think somebody saw someone wandering about and the cry went up: 'There's the vampire!' That was it, that was the word to get off that wall quick and get away from it. I just remember scampering home to my mother. 'What's the matter with you?' she said, 'I've seen a vampire!' and I got a clout round the ear for my trouble. I didn't really know what a vampire was." No children had been reported missing. No-one had seen the monster. So, why had the story spread? Tam Smith was 7 when the supposed vampire stalked the land of the dead: "There was an old lady who used to carry two cats in a basket. She would go to the graveyard to get peace away from the kids and let her cats have a wander. But she was in there the night we went looking for it and people were involving the 'cat woman' with the iron man. It was a shame when you think about it. She was an eccentric with wiry hair, but we called her Tin Lizzie. She was the iron man's 'burd' (wife)." And as it spread, the legend grew. The blame for the vampire panic rampage was laid at the door of American horror comics, with the likes of *Tales From The Crypt*, *The Haunt of Fear* and *The Vault of Horror* becoming main targets. The government set up a commission to investigate the effect of comics on the development of young minds. Some expert witnesses argued that the comics should be banned as they caused this degenerate behaviour. In the House of Commons, others took the matter less seriously. One Scottish MP, Mr. John Rankin, asked for the Loch Ness Monster to be excluded from the ban as Nessie was a "verrey parfait gentil" monster. Britain duly passed the Children and Young Persons (Harmful Publications) Act 1955 which, for the first time, specifically banned the sale of magazines and comics portraying "incidents of a repulsive or horrible nature" to children.

US Woman Hit By Meteorite

Ann Hodges, 34, was napping under quilts on her couch in Sylacauga, Alabama, on 30th November 1954 when a 9lb meteorite came through the ceiling and bounced off a console radio before hitting her in the thigh. It left a deep bruise and brought her both local fame and a major legal dispute with her landlady. As the rock came through the roof of her property, the landlady thought she rightfully owned it. During the protracted legal dispute Ann reportedly used the space rock as a door stop. By the time the case was settled (by Ann purchasing the meteorite from her landlady) interest had waned and the rock was virtually

Ann Hodges with the meteorite
Image: © Alabama Museum of Natural History

worthless. She eventually donated it to a local museum. The truth of the matter was that the rock wasn't rare. Thousands of meteorites land on earth every year, but they generally don't hit people. Instead of fame and fortune the event ruined Ann's life. Between the protracted court battle with her landlady and the media attention, Hodges' mental and physical health went downhill. She separated from her husband and eventually died of kidney failure in a nursing home aged just 52. The meteorite did bring good fortune to one of her neighbours. Julius Kempis McKinney, a local farmer, found a chunk of the 'Hodges meteorite' that was less than half as big as the one that struck the woman it was then named after. McKinney told his postman, who helped him get a lawyer to negotiate the sale of his find. In the end, he made enough money to buy a house and a car.

Hodges remains the only well-documented case of somebody being hit by a meteorite. But humans have continued to be affected by space junk. In 1992, a meteorite blazed across the sky in Peekskill, New York, before striking a woman's parked car. The repair bill probably stung a bit, but she wasn't injured in the strike. In 2003, a 40lb meteorite crashed through the roof of another home, this time in New Orleans, though luckily no one was hurt. And in 2007, a meteorite strike made people sick in Peru when it released arsenic fumes from an underground water source. The most spectacular meteor strike of modern times

The rock bounced off a Philco radio onto Ann Hodges
Image: © Alabama Museum of Natural History

occurred in the Ural Mountain region of Russia in 2013. The Chelyabinsk meteor, estimated to initially weigh about 12,000 tonnes and measure 66 feet wide, entered the Earth's atmosphere at a hypersonic speed of at least 33,000 mph and broke into pieces about 18-32 miles above the ground, It shattered countless windows and injured around 1200 people causing $33 million in damage. Devastating though it was, unlike Ann Hodges, no one was directly hit by fragments of the space rock.

Tragedy Leads To An Unsolved Mystery

On the 6th January 1954, a twin-engined Vickers Valetta WJ474 training aircraft of No.2 Air Navigation School Royal Air Force crashed near RAF Bovingdon just after take-off in snowy weather. The plane was carrying 17 passengers, despite having only 16 passenger seats. Everybody on the flight, except for the pilot, had just played a Rugby match at RAF Halton. The Valetta was seen to climb to about 400 feet then lose altitude during a turn to the left. It hit a tree five miles north of the

A Valetta T3 similar to the WJ474 which crashed

airfield and crashed near Tom's Hill, Aldbury, on part of the estate of the National Trust Ashridge Park property. The wreckage was strewn over two square miles. The combination of ice and snow on the ground and a narrow access road made rescue difficult. The National Trust chief ranger with four of his staff were first on the scene and reported: "Ten bodies were scattered about and we found two men alive. One was outside the aircraft and did not seen to be very badly hurt. The other was pulled from inside the smashed fuselage and was only semi-conscious". Of the two passengers who were rescued, one died later in hospital. All the others on board died at the scene. A subsequent investigation was unable to establish the cause of the accident, but the extra passenger and weather at take-off were found not to have contributed to the crash. An assumption was made that the pilot was trying to fly within sight of the ground in conditions of poor visibility, and that in doing so he crashed into the hill. Verdicts of accidental death were returned for the sixteen victims at the coroner's inquest held at Berkhamstead. The sole survivor, P/O P.D. Cliff, said at the inquest he could not remember anything after boarding the aircraft at Bovingdon. The coroner said that before the aircraft departed: "Certain things were not done which should have been done. But the question of taking off was entirely a matter for the pilot to decide. For some reason height was lost, no one knows why. No one will ever know what caused the unfortunate crash. There was nothing wrong with the engines." The sole survivor, Patrick Cliff, went on to have a distinguished career in the RAF retiring as a Wing Commander and was awarded an OBE for his service.

Juliane Koepcke pictured in 2019

One of the most famous sole survivors in history was born on 10th October 1954. Juliane Koepcke was seventeen at the time when she accompanied her zoologist parents to Peru. On Christmas eve 1971, a plane carrying the family and over eighty other passengers was caught in a violent storm. Juliane was thrown from the plane and descended 10,000ft, still strapped to her seat. She escaped with relatively minor injuries, all of the others on board were killed. After regaining consciousness, she remembered her father's advice to follow a river downstream to find help. After an incredible eleven day journey, she eventually found civilisation.

The South Goodwin Lightship

The world's first light vessel commenced operations in the River Thames back in 1734. Until as recently as the second half of the 20th century, all British light vessels were permanently manned. It's no surprise that lighthouse organisations around the world considered the life of a crewman stationed on board a lightship to be the one of the most dangerous jobs in the business. This in no small part is due to the fact that a lightship is not permitted to leave its station regardless of the weather. Lightships were used in locations where it was too dangerous or impracticable to build a lighthouse. This treacherous role led to a number of accidents involving light vessels over the years. In 1934, the Nantucket Lightship LV117 based off Nantucket Island off the northeastern coast of the USA was unintentionally rammed by the RMS Olympic liner and sank, killing some of its crew members. Also, off the northeast coast of the USA near Cuttyhunk, Massachusetts, the Vineyard Lightship was sunk by a

The Nantucket Lightship LV117 pictured in 1931

hurricane in September 1944, killing every member of the crew. In 1954, a 22-year-old British Ministry of Agriculture employee named Ronald Murton was sent to study bird migration off the coast of Kent in the UK. To do this, he joined the crew of the South Goodwin lightship which was anchored near the Goodwin Sands. Little did he know that his life was about to be literally turned upside down after only a month on board the ship. On the night of the 26th November 1954. the South Goodwin Lightship's anchor chains failed due to a hurricane force 12 storm. Now adrift, she was at the mercy of the swollen seas. The frightened crew sought refuge in the galley whilst the captain headed to the radio room to call for help. Suddenly, the vessel crashed into a sandbank and rolled violently onto her starboard side. This trapped the crew beneath the now submerged galley door. Ronald Morton managed to climb up to a hatch and escape. However, he was far from safe. Ronald was now precariously clinging to the upturned hull in storm force winds. The nearby North Goodwin lightship had raised the alarm, but lifeboats were unable to reach the site due to the weather and were forced to turn back. With his life ebbing away after over 8 hours on the hull, a USAF search and rescue helicopter from Manston Air Force Base managed to drop a line to Ronald and winch him to safety. He had survived, but only just. During his time on the hull, Ronald remembers hearing a tapping sound coming from within, suggesting some of his crew mates were still alive. However, it would take a further 18 hours before the storm abated allowing divers to reach the vessel. Tragically no bodies were ever found suggesting the rest of the crew had drowned and been washed out to sea. The helicopter crew received medals for their bravery in saving Ronald's life that night.

Pictured at low tide, the South Goodwin laid on her side
Image courtesy of Lighthouse Digest

The 1954 World Cup Final

When the USA beat England 1-0 at the 1950 World Cup in Brazil, football fans thought that they had witnessed the biggest upset they would ever see. Four years later the World Cup Final in Bern, Switzerland would see a result that would turn all known football form on its head. West Germany, as it was then, still recovering from the ravages of war barely had a national league and was made up of part-timers. As Ferenc Puskas lined up for the final, the world's greatest footballer at the time stood opposite a man trained as a banker who also ran a laundrette. The West German captain Fritz Walter and his team had overcome giant odds just to be at

The Hungarian World Cup Team

The West German World Cup Team

the Wankdorf Stadium. Few gave them any chance against the Mighty Magyars of Hungary, who were unbeaten in four years. Hungary had outclassed England 6-3 and 7-1 in the months before the World Cup and carried that high-scoring form into the tournament. Without the star power of their competitors, West Germany had to find a different way to win. Coach Sepp Herberger, who had been in charge since before World War II, set about forging a tight-knit squad. Herberger relied heavily on 1953 German champions Kaiserslautern to form his squad's core. From there, the coach added players whom he felt would add to the team spirit. That included the left field choice of Helmut Rahn, a former coal worker whose outgoing personality was anything but professional but lightened the camp's mood. The Hungarians, who had already beaten the West Germans 8-3 in the group stages, started brightly and raced into a two-nil lead after just eight minutes. Everything seemed to be going to script. Puskas tapped home the first when a deflected shot fell kindly to him, and Czibor nipped in to score the second after Werner Kohlmeyer's dreadful back pass to goalkeeper Toni Turek. Rather than stun the Germans, the setback spurred them into action. Forward Max Morlock famously screamed "Now let's show them!". In the 10th minute, Rahn whizzed in a low, speculative shot-cum-cross from the left and Morlock was on hand to slide the ball home. And after just 18 minutes, the scores were level at 2-2. Rahn ghosted in at the far post from a corner to half-volley the ball home

Hungary celebrate their first goal

with an outstretched foot. A Hungarian onslaught ensued, as Turek denied Hidegkuti twice, the Magyars hit the woodwork three times and Kohlmeyer made up for his first-half error by clearing off the line. Step forward, Rahn, one of the original bad boys of football whom Herberger had elevated to the first 11. On 84 minutes, he collected possession at the top of the box, feigned to shoot with his right before cutting back onto his left and nestling a low effort into the corner of the net. In the words of one commentator: "Drei zu zwei führt Deutschland! Halten Sie mich für verrückt, halten Sie mich für übergeschnappt!" ("Germany lead 3-2! Call me mad, call me crazy!"). It's a line that resonates in German football culture to this day. There was still time for a Puskas disallowed goal for offside and another outstanding Turek save from Kocsis in the dying minutes, but West Germany were world champions, against all the odds.

In July 1954, Maureen Connolly beat fellow American Louise Brough 6-2,7-5 to win her third Wimbledon Ladies' Singles title in a row. But that was not the biggest tennis story of the year. On 20th July 1954, Connolly broke her leg in an accident in which she was hit by a truck while horse riding. This injury put an end to the career of the rising star, which probably changed tennis history. 'Little Mo', aged just 19 at the time, had already claimed nine Grand Slam titles and had become the first female player to win the Grand Slam (four major events in the same season) in the previous year, losing only one set in the process. To go with those stats Connolly, since her loss in the second round of the US Championships in 1950 at the age of 15, had never again been defeated in a Grand Slam tournament thus holding a 52-2 record. There is little doubt that without this tragic accident Maureen Connolly would have won many more titles and could have become the greatest player of all time. Connolly was born in 1934 in San Diego, California. Her first passion was horse riding, but as her family could not afford the lessons, she took up tennis. Connolly hit powerful ground strokes with great accuracy, especially on her backhand side. At the age of 11, she was given the nickname 'Little Mo' by a San Diego sportswriter, in comparison with the firepower of a US Navy ship, the

Maureen 'Little Mo' Connolly

USS Missouri, known as 'Big Mo'. Starting in 1951, Little Mo dominated the game to an unbelievable extent. She triumphed in all of the nine Grand Slam tournaments that she competed in: the US Nationals (1951, 1952, 1953), the Australian Open (1953), Roland Garros (1953, 1954) and Wimbledon (1952, 1953, 1954). In July 1954, Connolly had just defended her title at the All England Club, and it seemed that no one could prevent her from extending her list of achievements, especially considering that she was only 19 years old. On that fateful day in July, Connolly jumped on the back of her horse, Colonel Merryboy, which she had been given two years before winning her first Wimbledon title and went on a ride which ended tragically at 1.30pm with a terrible accident. Despite all her efforts such as attending ballet classes to regain her strength, Little Mo was never able to recover her full capacities. In January 1955, during an exhibition match she felt a shooting pain in her leg while running to get a drop shot. With great sadness, Connolly announced her retirement from tennis, at the age of 20. She died tragically young aged just 34, suffering from ovarian cancer.

Jaroslav Drobný

Wimbledon 1954

The Mens' Singles title at Wimbledon was won by Jaroslav Drobný who beat Ken Rosewall 13-11, 4-6, 6-2, 9-7 in an epic final. Though born in Czechoslovakia, Drobný travelled under an Egyptian passport, making him the first and, thus far, only African citizen to win the tournament.

The First Rugby League World Cup

Contested between France (hosts), Great Britain, Australia and New Zealand (The USA were invited, but cancelled)

The Rugby League World Cup was first played in France in 1954. But, if 10 years previously, you'd asked any French player taking part in that inaugural competition whether they'd ever foresee playing a World Cup on home soil they'd have laughed in your face. And that's because during the war, in Nazi-controlled France, rugby league was illegal. But why? It seems a preposterous notion today. Who would outlaw an entire sport, and on what possible basis? The first rugby league match played in France was an exhibition game between England and Australia in Paris in 1933. Until that point, all rugby clubs in France had been playing rugby union. Ten thousand spectators turned up, among them Jean Galia, a player with the Villeneuve club. He liked what he saw and gathered together a team of players who 10 weeks later arrived in England to play their first matches of rugby league. But then came the Second World War, and France's Nazi puppet state of Vichy. This German-backed government, stacked with former rugby union figures and beholden to the establishment, took its revenge. Under the

Sam Smith, David Valentine (captain) and John Thorley collect the trophy for the GB team

pretext of reasserting 'traditional values', rugby league was deemed likely to contaminate the nation's youth and declared 'morally decrepit'. Marshal Petain, the collaborationist leader of the Vichy government, signed the decree proscribing rugby league on 19th December 1941. It was the first and only sport anywhere to be banned during the war. Back to 1954 and against all expectations, Great Britain topped the round-robin table alongside France. The two would meet in the final at the Parc des Princes in Paris. "We really couldn't believe we made it," said the GB coach Valentine. "Maybe it was because there was no weight of expectation on us, we could play freely." On 13th November, only two days after both teams had played their last qualifying match, a packed stadium saw a tense final that see-sawed either way but, despite a valiant French fightback late in the game, stand-off Gordon Brown's second try of the match was enough for Great Britain to prevail 16-12. As journalist Alfred Drewry wrote: "There is no spectacle in sport more stirring than that of a team accomplishing more than theoretically it should be capable of." It was also a triumph for France as huge crowds flocked to see a sport that had been banned until their liberation. The match had been televised in the UK, allowing millions of new TV owners who had bought sets the previous year to watch the coronation of Elizabeth II to witness the first British team in any sport to be crowned winners of a World Cup.

Rugby Union

England missed out on a seventh Grand Slam when they lost 11-3 to France at the Stade Colombes near Paris. This allowed Wales to claim the Five Nations Championship on points difference.

1954 Wisden Cricketers of the Year

The key factor in Pakistan's unexpected victory over England at The Oval in 1954 was the medium-fast bowling of vice-captain **Fazal Mahmood**, who took twelve wickets for 99 runs. That was only one of Fazal's consistently good performances in England which earned him exceedingly high praise. Known as 'The Alec Bedser of Pakistan', Fazal fully lived up to his reputation. In first-class matches he headed the Pakistan bowling averages with 77 wickets at 17.53 runs each with his 20 Test wicket haul being more than double the next best for Pakistan. For his part in Pakistan drawing the series he received a Cup and a cheque for his Oval Test achievement, judged the finest individual feat of the season. And he was selected as the first Pakistan player in Wisden's Five Cricketers of the Year. In build, run-up and bowling action, Fazal did not resemble Bedser, but their bowling methods bore a distinct similarity. Both concentrated on varied swing and a mixture of leg-cutters and break-backs at just above medium-pace; both were masters of length bowling, stifling the batting and forcing mistakes.

Fazal Mahmood

Awarded in 1955 for performances in 1954, the other 4 Wisden Cricketers of the Year were:

Bruce Dooland, an Australian, who did much to restore right-arm leg-break and googly bowling to an important place in the strategy of the game when, in his first two seasons in English first-class cricket, he took 368 wickets (172, average 16.58, in 1953, and 196, average 15.48, in 1954).

Eric Hollies also had a fine season with the ball, but is best remembered for an event some six years earlier. When Donald Bradman walked to the wicket at Kennington Oval in August 1948, to play his last Test innings before retirement, he received one of the most tumultuous receptions known in cricket. A moment later the vast crowd sent up a united gasp of amazement as they saw Australia's champion bowled second ball by Hollies without scoring. Hollies will forever be remembered as the man who denied Bradman the four runs he needed to end his test career averaging over 100 runs.

Brian Statham established himself on the unfriendly pitches of the West Indies in the early months of 1954. He headed the Test averages with 16 wickets at 28.75 runs apiece and his opening spell at Georgetown, in which he dismissed Worrell, Stollmeyer and Walcott for ten runs, played a leading part in England's Third Test victory by nine wickets.

The fifth Cricketer of the Year was the Australian **George Edward Tribe**. In his eight full seasons at Northampton, he did the 1,000 runs-100 wickets double seven times, and in 1955 took 176 wickets. His team-mate, wicket-keeper Keith Andrew, called him "probably the best cricketer I ever played with". England fast bowler Frank Tyson described the fact that Tribe only played three tests for Australia as "criminal".

Lester Piggott's Eventful Year

To say that Lester Piggott had a mixed year in 1954 is something of an understatement. Early in the season he won the Epsom Derby but at Royal Ascot his career was nearly ended. The youngster was fourth choice to partner Never Say Die, never again would Lester find himself so far down the pecking order at Derby time but he got the ride. He cut down his 21 rivals as swiftly and effectively as he would, famously, cut his lawn that evening. It was the first entry on an incomparable roll of honour: 9 Derbys and a record 30 British Classics in all. But in the short time that Lester had been riding he had made enemies in high places, with disapproval expressed by senior figures of the sport who thought him brash, disrespectful and dangerous. He had already served several suspensions, generally for careless riding. It is distinctly possible the top brass were simply waiting for a suitable opportunity to cut Piggott, the tall poppy, down to size. When Lester lined up on the Derby winner in the King Edward VII stakes at the Royal Ascot meeting, a bold run was expected. It turned out to be a very rough race. As the field turned for home with Blue Prince II and Arabian Night leading the way,

Lester Piggott

those in behind prepared to deliver their challenges. Sir Gordon Richards, riding Rashleigh, came round the bend with two horses between him and the rail, namely Garter (ridden by Lester's cousin Bill Rickaby) and Dragon Fly (Doug Smith). Lester and Never Say Die were just behind. As they straightened up, Rashleigh came slightly wide as did Garter next to him, creating space on the inside. Lester spied a gap between Garter and Dragon Fly and drove Never Say Die into it, making a line of four. Just at that moment Richards tried to correct the drifting Rashleigh by pulling him back towards the rail, and in so doing he came across Garter,

Never Say Die

bumping him hard more than once. Never Say Die, who habitually lugged to the left, did so again under pressure and bumped Garter on his other side. The stewards initially blamed Richards for the interference, but the other senior jockeys closed ranks and supported Richards who had been knighted by the Queen a year earlier. The Jockey Club then stripped Lester of his licence and set no time limit on his sentence, suggesting he might consider reapplying after six months. Furthermore, in an act of astonishingly petty vindictiveness, he was also required to leave home and work away from his father Keith's yard. The verdict was received by Lester with barely stifled fury and by the racing public with vociferous outrage. As the months passed a degree of common sense prevailed. In late September, by which time coincidentally or not, Richards had retired. The Jockey Club informed Lester that he could reapply for his licence. This he did, and his request was granted. His first ride back at Newmarket was a winner.

Sir Gordon Richards as depicted on a Gallaher's cigarette card

The Four Minute Mile

Two years previously at the 1952 Olympics in Helsinki, Roger Bannister suffered a big disappointment just missing out on a medal by finishing 4th. However it was this that strengthened, not weakened his resolve to achieve something truly memorable. The four minute mile had long been the Holy Grail of men's athletics and many had come close. The last Englishman to hold the world record for the mile was Sidney Wooderson, with a time of 4min. 6.4sec. set in London in 1937. Since that time, there were five improvements by the two Swedish athletes Gunder Haegg and Arne Andersson, with Haegg holding the current official world record of 4min. 1.4sec. Roger Bannister, aged 25, became the first man to run a mile in less than four minutes. His time at the Iffley Road track, Oxford, in the annual match between the Amateur Athletic Association and Oxford University, was 3min. 59.4sec. Bannister, a former president of the Oxford club and now a medical student nearing qualification, ran as first string for the visiting side against his old university. The race was carefully planned and Bannister received considerable assistance from the intelligent pace-making of Chris Brasher, a former Cambridge runner (who would later go on to set up the London Marathon in 1981). Brasher led the field through the first quarter mile in 57.3sec. and reached the half-mile in 1min.

Bannister at the finish line of the historic race

58sec. with Bannister three yards behind him. From there, Christopher Chataway (who had a subsequent career in broadcasting and became Minister for Telecommunications in the Edward Heath Government) took up the lead and reached the three-quarter mile mark in 3min. 0.4sec., with Bannister at 3min. 0.7sec. Bannister took the lead with some 350 yards to go, passed one unofficial timekeeper at the 1,500-metre mark in 3min. 43sec., equalling the world's record for that distance, and thereafter, throwing in all his reserves, he broke the tape in 3min. 59.4sec. The afternoon had been squally, but just before the race, which started at 6pm, the weather relented slightly. Nonetheless, conditions were far from ideal. After the news that a world record had been broken and a great athletic landmark passed, there was pandemonium among the spectators. Bannister seemed a shoe-in for the very first Sport's Personality of the Year Award. Votes were made by postcard and after the 14,500 votes had been counted the winner was .... Christopher Chataway. Sports Illustrated, a new magazine in America, did however give their Athlete of the Year Award to the man who broke the 4 minute mile. After retiring from athletics, Bannister became a leading neurologist publishing over eighty papers. In 2014, he said of his two careers "I'd rather be remembered for my work in neurology than my running. If you offered me the chance to make a great breakthrough in the study of the autonomic nervous system, I'd take that over the four minute mile right away. I worked in medicine for sixty years. I ran for about eight."

Rocky Marciano Vs Ezzard Charles | The Rematch

17th September 1954 at the Yankee Stadium in New York

On 17th June 1954 Marciano and Charles fought a bruising 15 round bout which Marciano won on a unanimous points decision. A re-match was called for and it duly took place on 17th September 1954 at the Yankee Stadium, New York. It was one of the greatest fights in heavyweight history and was voted Ring magazine's fight of the year. Charles won the first round by landing some clean punches on Marciano's jaw. In the second round, Marciano hit Charles with a body blow and then knocked him down on the canvas. Marciano now went in for the kill, but Charles proved too slippery and survived the round. The fight then became an offensive–defensive affair with Marciano constantly on the attack and Charles content to do defensive boxing while throwing only occasional punches. The two fighters could not keep the action up and the pace dipped with the excitement coming from Marciano's use of roughhouse tactics like throwing low blows and hitting after the bell. The fouls did not affect the judges who had Marciano well ahead after the fifth round. Something strange happened in the sixth because of which

Rocky Marciano

Ezzard Charles almost won the fight. As Charles and Marciano emerged from a clinch towards the end of the round, Marciano was seen sporting a deep wound on his left nostril. It was unclear how he had got hurt with some claiming it was due to Charles's punches, and Marciano laying the blame on Charles's elbow. Marciano now started bleeding profusely from the wound; he would later observe: "I knew something was wrong because the blood was running like from a faucet." Meanwhile, Charles's corner was feeling triumphant after the sixth; Charles was advised by them to keep throwing punches at Marciano's nose. In the seventh, Marciano went out with a makeshift patch over his nose, but the device was quickly knocked off by Charles's punches. Remarkably enough, Marciano won the seventh by landing more blows than Charles who was left staggering at the end of the round. Even so, it was Marciano who was in danger because of the nose wound which continued to gush blood. Word reached Rocky's corner that the fight would only be allowed to continue for at most two more rounds. In the interval before the eighth, Marciano's corner advised him to go after Charles's body. Instead, he decided to ignore the advice and

Ezzard Charles

went after his opponent's head. As Marciano later explained "I was spilling too much blood, and they might have stopped it. I like my title too much to lose it on account of a little blood. I don't knock 'em out in the body. I knock 'em out on the chin." With 24 seconds left before the end of the eighth, Ezzard Charles was knocked out by Marciano. Marciano's purse for the fight was around $250,000; this contrasted with the $6,000 Ed Furgol earned for his win in the 1954 US Open Golf Championship.

The Open Golf Championship

7th - 9th July 1954 at Royal Birkdale Golf Club in Southport, England

At Royal Birkdale in 1954, Peter Thomson became the first Australian to win The Open, beginning his dominant run at golf's oldest major. Jim Ferrier, at the 1947 PGA Championship, was the only other Australian-born player to have won one of golf's major tournaments. The Royal Birkdale course had been brought up to Open standard in 1935 with plans to host The Open in 1940. However, this was cancelled due to the war. It finally made its debut 14 years later. Thomson simply dominated The Open; he was sixth on debut in 1951 and then was a runner-up for the next two years. His victory at Birkdale was the first of three in a row, with five in all. At this year's tournament, American Ben Hogan had decided not travel back to Britain to defend his title. With a round to play, fellow countryman and three-time champion golfer Bobby Locke was two strokes behind the trio of Thomson, Englishman Syd Scott and Welshman Dai Rees. Scott, from what is now Cumbria, set a new course record of 67 in the second round and closed with a 72 to set the target at 284. Rees could not get up and down at the

Peter Thomson (right) and his caddy

last, so also had a 72. This would be the second of three runner-up finishes for the Welshman. Thomson found himself on the steep slope of a bunker at the 16th, 25 yards from the flag. With his feet together in an awkward stance and his eyes closed, he thumped the ball high in the air and it stuck virtually where it landed just inches from the hole. "That won it for me, no doubt." he said. "Had I made a mess of that one, I'd have been a goner." The 24-year-old was also in a bunker at the last, but a 71 put him one ahead on 283. Locke managed a 70 but could only join the other runners-up.

David James 'Dai' Rees

Dai Rees may have been considered the nearly man of British golf were it not for his astounding record in the Ryder Cup. Not only did he play in nine Ryder Cups, but he captained the side on no fewer than five occasions leading the team to victory in 1957. This was an incredible achievement as the cup was then a contest between Britain and Ireland and The United States. The tournament was a mismatch in terms of resources and the Americans had last lost the cup in 1933. 1957 was to be the last time the cup would be won this side of the pond until 1985, by which time Europe had joined Britain and Ireland to make the competition more evenly balanced. Soon after the famous victory in 1957, Rees was appointed Commander of the Order of the British Empire and also won the coveted BBC Sports Personality of the Year award.

The first prototype AEC Routemaster bus was completed in September 1954. It was designed by London Transport and has since become a British design classic alongside the red telephone box, the Mini, Concorde and the Supermarine Spitfire. Of the 2,876 Routemasters built, 1,280 are still in existence. They last saw regular service in London in 2005.

This British Rail Standard Class 8 steam locomotive was built in 1954. Named the Duke of Gloucester, it replaced the locomotive destroyed in the horrific rail crash at Harrow and Wealdstone in 1952. It was the only Class 8 ever built. In service for only 8 years, it was beset with performance issues. It was bought and restored by enthusiasts in 1974.

The Lockheed C-130 Hercules first flew on the 29th August 1954. It went to become one of the most successful military aircraft ever built. The versatile air frame was originally intended for troop and cargo transport. With over 2,500 built, it has also been used for weather reconnaissance, aerial refuelling, search and rescue and airborne assault.

The Sikorsky H-34 'Choctaw' piston-engined military helicopter first flew on the 8th March 1954. The Westland Aircraft manufacturer in the UK acquired a licence to the H-34. They adapted the helicopter to turbine power producing it under the name of the Westland Wessex. It would be used by the Royal Navy, the Royal Air Force and for search and rescue.

Patented in Germany in 1954 by inventor Gottlob Widmann, the Wigomat was one of the world's first electrical drip coffee makers. Up until the 1950's, coffee was brewed by hand or by using a percolator. Both methods were criticised for overheating the coffee. The Wigomat was promoted as brewing the coffee at the perfect temperature.

image courtesy: www.earlytelevision.org

The RCA CT-100 was the world's first mass produced colour television. It first went on sale in April 1954 in the USA. It cost $1000 which was about half the cost of a reasonably priced car. When launched, the screen was only 11.5" across. However, by the end of the year RCA launched an improved model with a 21" screen. Around 150 survive to this day.

The iconic Fender Stratocaster was launched in 1954. Designed by Leo Fender and his team, it was revolutionary and has become a gold standard in electric guitar design. The body with its double cutaway and contoured back was designed for comfort whilst playing standing up with a strap. Its three pickups and vibrato arm also make it incredibly versatile.

The Hammond B-3 organ is another iconic instrument much loved by musicians to this day. Launched in 1954, it is an evolution of the original Hammond organ designed by Laurens Hammond and John M. Hanert in 1935. Its distinctive sound is produced by tone wheels, not pipes and the use of drawbars allows players to shape its sound in real-time.

The iconic Mercedes-Benz 300 SL, with its gullwing doors, was launched in 1954. It was produced as a coupé until 1957, then as a roadster until 1963. The SL denotes 'super-leicht' meaning 'super light'. With a 3-litre straight six engine and 4 speed manual transmission it was capable of 263km/h (163mph). It was the world's fastest production car of its time.

In 1954, Jaguar Cars launched the Jaguar D-Type racing car with the specific goal of winning the Le Mans 24-hour race. The designers drew on aeronautical technology to incorporate a revolutionary aluminium monocoque construction to the driver's cockpit. The D-type achieved its goal by winning three consecutive Le Mans races in 1955, 1956 and 1957.

The Kodak Stereo Camera was launched in 1954. It was a 35mm film camera with twin lenses capable of taking two pictures of a scene. The specially processed film could then be viewed in a dedicated Kodak viewer to give the impression of a 3D image. It sold for $84.50 and sold about 100,000 units between 1954 and 1959.

Launched in 1954, the Leica M3 35mm rangefinder camera would go on to be a classic. By many accounts, it is the best camera of all time. It would also go on to be Leica's best-selling camera of all time. Many M3's from the era are still in perfect working order today. In 2019. a pre-series model (effectively a prototype) was sold at auction for 360,000 Euros.

Photo Credits

Credits shown in the order in which they appear in the book. Photos not listed are in the public domain.

Key to page numbers

fc = front cover; **ifc** = inside front cover; **tp** = title page; **cp** = contents page; **ap1** = acknowledgements page 1; **ap2** = acknowledgements page 2; **ibc** = inside back cover; **bc** = back cover; **3** = page 3; **4** = page 4; etc.

Key to object position on page

tl = top left; *t* = top; *tc* = top centre; *tr* = top right; *cla* = centre left above; *ca* = centre above; *cra* = centre right above; *cl* = centre left; *c* = centre; *cr* = centre right; *clb* = centre left below; *cb* = centre below; *crb* = centre right below; *bl* = bottom left; *b* = bottom; *bc* = bottom centre; *br* = bottom right; *w* = whole page; *h* = header; *tb* = text background

Key to image licence types

CC BY-SA 2.0 = https://creativecommons.org/licenses/by-sa/2.0/deed.en;
CC BY-SA 3.0 = https://creativecommons.org/licenses/by-sa/3.0/deed.en;
CC BY-SA 4.0 = https://creativecommons.org/licenses/by-sa/4.0/deed.en;
(m) = image has been modified as permitted under licensing terms

fc *cra*: Prince Philip (m) © Archives New Zealand, Wikimedia Commons, CC BY-SA 2.0; **tp** *w*: Mercedes-Benz 300 SL (m) © Wolfgang on adobestock.com; **2** *tc*: Walt Disney and Wernher von Braun, © James Vaughan and Nick Derrington, Flickr.com, CC BY-SA 2.0; **2** *tr*: Loading airplane © Dick Gilbert, Flickr.com, CC BY-SA 2.0; **3** *tl*: Queen Elizabeth visit © State Records of SA, Flickr.com, CC BY-SA 2.0; **5** *cla*: Roger Bannister, © KEYSTONE Pictures USA / Alamy Stock Photo; **16** *cla*: Oprah Winfrey © INTX: The Internet & Television Expo, Wikimedia Commons, CC BY-SA 2.0; **16** *clb*: Iain Banks © Pasi Välkkynen, Wikimedia Commons, CC BY-SA 2.0; **17** *cla*: Michael Holding © Sanjiva Persad, Wikimedia Commons, CC BY-SA 2.0; **17** *clb*: John Travolta © Vegafi, Wikimedia Commons, CC BY-SA 3.0; **18** *cla*: Anish Kapoor © Vogler, Wikimedia Commons, CC BY-SA 4.0; **18** *clb*: Jackie Chan © Gage Skidmore, Wikimedia Commons, CC BY-SA 3.0; **19** *cla*: Trevor Francis © Christophe95, Wikimedia Commons, CC BY-SA 3.0; **19** *clb*: Jerry Seinfeld © David Shankbone , Wikimedia Commons, CC BY-SA 3.0; **22** *cla*: Neil Tennant © Eva Rinaldi, Wikimedia Commons, CC BY-SA 2.0; **20** *clb*: Angela Merkel © Raimond Spekking , Wikimedia Commons, CC BY-SA 4.0; **21** *cla*: James Cameron © Angela George, Wikimedia Commons, CC BY-SA 3.0; **21** *clb*: Elvis Costello © Matt Johnson , Wikimedia Commons, CC BY-SA 2.0; **22** *cla*: Adam Ant © Peter Chiapperino, Wikimedia Commons, CC BY-SA 3.0; **23** *cla*: Denzel Washington © Georges Biard, Wikimedia Commons, CC BY-SA 3.0; **23** *clb row 1*: Howard Stern © Bill Norton, Wikimedia Commons, CC BY-SA 2.0; **23** *cb row 1*: Matt Groening © Gage Skidmore, Wikimedia Commons, CC BY-SA 2.0; **23** *crb row 1*: Rene Russo © John Mathew Smith & www.celebrity-photos.com, Wikimedia Commons, CC BY-SA 2.0; **23** *clb row 2*: Anthony Head © pinguino k, Wikimedia Commons, CC BY-SA 2.0; **23** *cb row 2*: Ron Howard © David Shankbone, Wikimedia Commons, CC BY-SA 3.0; **23** *crb row 2*: Jane Campion © New Zealand Government, Office of the Governor-General, Wikimedia Commons, CC BY-SA 4.0; **23** *clb row 3*: Jim Belushi © COD Newsroom, Wikimedia Commons, CC BY-SA 2.0; **23** *cb row 3*: Kathleen Turner © Kingkongphoto & www.celebrity-photos.com, Wikimedia Commons, CC BY-SA 2.0; **23** *crb row 3*: Cherie Blair © Foreign and Commonwealth Office, Wikimedia Commons, CC BY-SA 1.0; **23** *clb row 4*: Sam Allerdyce © Brian Minkoff-London Pixels, Wikimedia Commons, CC BY-SA 4.0; **23** *cb row 4*: Ang Lee © nicolas genin, Wikimedia Commons, CC BY-SA 2.0; **23** *crb row 4*: Lee Child © Mark Coggins, Wikimedia Commons, CC BY-SA 2.0; **23** *clb row 5*: Ross Brawn © fry_theonly, Wikimedia Commons, CC BY-SA 2.0; **23** *cb row 5*: Ray Liotta © Georges Biard, Wikimedia Commons, CC BY-SA 3.0; **23** *crb row 5*: Chris Evert © glennia, Flickr.com, CC BY-SA 2.0; **27** *tl*: Coins © Jo Smiley Hailey, Unsplash.com; **27** *tr*: House © Sludgegulper, Wikimedia Commons, CC BY-SA 2.0; **27** *cal*: Ford Anglia © Charles01, Wikimedia Commons, CC BY-SA 3.0; **27** *bl*: Bush TV © Thngs, Flickr.com, CC BY-SA 2.0; **27** *bc*: Bread © Dmitry Makeev, Wikimedia Commons, CC BY-SA 4.0; **27** *br*: Petrol pump © Erik Mclean, Unsplash.com; **29** *tr*: Office © Huppertsberg, Wikimedia Commons, CC BY-SA 3.0; **35** *tr*: Lucienne Day © The Robin and Lucienne Day Foundation - Photographer: Studio Briggs, Wikimedia Commons, CC BY-SA 4.0; **36** *c*: Coronation Chicken © Brent Hofacker, Shutterstock.com; **39** *ca*: Cake © Kimberly Vardeman, Wikimedia Commons, CC BY-SA 2.0; **38** *tl*: Bikini Model © Harry Pot / Anefo, Wikimedia Commons, CC BY-SA 4.0; **38** *br*: Model © Jenny Freebairn; **39** *tl*: Seaside Models © Hans Pinn, Wikimedia Commons, CC BY-SA 3.0; **39** *tr*: Audrey Hepburn © Hans Gerber, Wikimedia Commons, CC BY-SA 4.0; **39** *bl*: Couple © daves_archive1, Flickr.com, CC BY-SA 2.0; **40** *tr*: Swimming Pool Model © Fritz Cohen, Flickr.com, CC BY-SA 3.0; **42** *br*: The National Gallery (m) © Uukgoblin, Wikimedia Commons, CC BY-SA 3.0; **44** *clb*: Alistair Sim, © PA Images / Alamy Stock Photo; **45** *clb*: Charles Laughton, © BRITISH LION FILM CORP\STUDIOCANAL/RAY HEARNE, Alamy Stock Photo; **46** *crb*: Moira Lister & Tony Hancock, © PA Images / Alamy Stock Photo; **47** *tr*: Dylan Thomas, © Rollie McKenna/ Science History Images / Alamy Stock Photo; **48** *clb*: Zoo Quest, © PA Images / Alamy Stock Photo; **49** *tl*: 1984, © TCD/Prod.DB / Alamy Stock Photo; **49** *clb*: Running Wild, © Pictorial Press Ltd / Alamy Stock Photo; **51** *clb* & **53** *bl*: Vera Lynn © Eric Koch / Anefo, Wikimedia Commons, CC BY-SA 3.0; **53** *tl*: Eddie Calvert © Bradford Timeline, Flickr.com, CC BY-SA 2.0; **54** *t*: King's College Chapel © Flcherb, Wikimedia Commons, CC BY-SA 3.0; **55** *cl*: Jimmy Edwards © CHRIS SHAW, Wikimedia Commons, CC BY-SA 3.0; **57** *tl*: Ring © Peter J. Yost, Wikimedia Commons, CC BY-SA 4.0; **57,59** *tl* & **57,58,59** *cl* & **57,58,59** *bl*: Created with the assistance of DALL-E 3/ Adobe Photoshop; **59** *tl*: Conch Shell © arbyreed, Flickr.com, CC BY-SA 2.0; **60** *tr*: Reclining Figure © Andrew Dunn, Wikimedia Commons, CC BY-SA 2.0; **60** *cra*: Single Form © Andy Scott, Wikimedia Commons, CC BY-SA 4.0; **60** *br*: Corinthos © Rept0n1x, Wikimedia Commons, CC BY-SA 3.0; **61** *tl*: John Masefield © Los Angeles Times, Wikimedia Commons, CC BY-SA 4.0; **61** *br*: Carol Ann Duffy © walnut whippet, Wikimedia Commons, CC BY-SA 2.0; **62** *bl*: Radio © Joe Haupt, Wikimedia Commons, CC BY-SA 2.0; **63** *bl*: Grinder © Hustvedt, Wikimedia Commons, CC BY-SA 3.0; **64** *bl*: Obninsk plant © RIA Novosti archive, image #409173 / Pavel Bykov, Wikimedia Commons, CC BY-SA 3.0; **65** *bl*: Large Hadron Collider © Tighef, Wikimedia Commons, CC BY-SA 3.0; **66** *tr*: Kidney transplant © Wiremu Stadtwald Demchick, Wikimedia Commons, CC BY-SA 3.0; **66** *bl*: Thomas Francis Jr. © Wellcome Images, Wikimedia Commons, CC BY-SA 4.0; **68** *bl*: Turing plaque © Joseph Birr-Pixton, Wikimedia Commons, CC BY-SA 3.0; **70** *tr*: K2 © Kuno Lechner, Wikimedia Commons, CC BY-SA 3.0; **71** *tr*: Blons village © böhringer friedrich, Wikimedia Commons, CC BY-SA 2.5; **71** *br*: Post avalanche © Helmut Klapper, Vorarlberger Landesbibliothek, Wikimedia Commons, CC BY-SA 4.0; **72** *t*: Glasgow Southern Necropolis gatehouse © AlistairMcMillan, Wikimedia Commons, CC BY-SA 4.0; **73** *tr*: Ann Hodges © Alabama Museum of Natural History, www.almnh.museums.ua.edu; **73** *br*: Meteorite © Alabama Museum of Natural History, www.almnh.museums.ua.edu; **74** *tr*: Vickers Valetta © RuthAS, Wikimedia Commons, CC BY-SA 3.0; **74** *bl*: Juliane Koepcke © Cancillería del Perú, Wikimedia Commons, CC BY-SA 3.0; **75** *br*: South Goodwin Lightship © Lighthouse Digest, www.lighthousedigest.com; **76** *cla*: Hungarian team © Fortepan adományozó MAGYAR HÍREK FOLYÓIRAT, Wikimedia Commons, CC BY-SA 3.0; *continued on next page...*

Photo Credits continued

76 *crb*: Goal celebration © ETH-Bibliothek Zürich, Bildarchiv / Fotograf: Comet Photo AG (Zürich) , Wikimedia Commons, CC BY-SA 4.0; **78** *cra*: Rugby League trophy © SuperStock / Alamy Stock Photo; **79** *cra*: Fazal Mahmood © PA Images / Alamy Stock Photo; **80** *clb*: Never Say Die © John Slusar, greyhoundderby.com; **80** *tr*: Lester Piggott © Ragge Strand, Bjørn Fjørtoft, Rolf Engesland, Wikimedia Commons, CC BY-SA 4.0; **81** *tr*: Roger Bannister © KEYSTONE Pictures USA / Alamy Stock Photo; **83** *tr*: Peter Thomson © Mercury newspaper/ Libraries Tasmania, Wikimedia Commons, CC BY-SA 3.0; **84** *t*: Routemaster (m) © Chris Sampson, Wikimedia Commons, CC BY-SA 2.0; **84** *b*: Duke of Gloucester train (m) © Hugh Llewelyn, Wikimedia Commons, CC BY-SA 2.0; **84** *t*: Routemaster (m) © Chris Sampson, Wikimedia Commons, CC BY-SA 2.0; **84** *b*: Duke of Gloucester train (m) © Hugh Llewelyn, Wikimedia Commons, CC BY-SA 2.0; **86** *t*: Wigomat coffee maker (m) © www.acosta.eu, Wikimedia Commons, CC BY-SA 3.0; **86** *b*: RCA CT-100 TV (m) © The Early Television Foundation / www.earlytelevision.org; **87** *b*: Hammond organ (m) © Museum of Making Music, Wikimedia Commons, CC BY-SA 3.0; **88** *t*: Mercedes-Benz 300 SL (m) © Ank kumar, Wikimedia Commons, CC BY-SA 4.0; **88** *b*: Jaguar D-Type (m) © Mr.choppers, Wikimedia Commons, CC BY-SA 3.0; **89** *t*: Kodak Stereo Camera (m) © John Alan Elson, Wikimedia Commons, CC BY-SA 4.0; **89** *b*: Leica M3 (m) © Hannes Grobe, Wikimedia Commons, CC BY-SA 3.0; **92** *tc*: Coffee Table (m) © Sincerely Media, Unsplash.com; **BC** *tl*: Cycle race (m) © Wim van Rossem for Anefo, Wikimedia Commons, CC BY-SA 3.0;

Graphic and Background Image Credits

Credits shown in the order in which they appear in the book.

Additional Key

(ic) = icon; (ph) = photo

fc *c*, **tp** *ca* & **bc**: (ph) Texture (m) © Felipe Santana, unsplash.com; **2-15**: (ph) Wood (m) © Michael Schwarzenberger, pixabay.com; **2-3, 16-91** *tb*: (ph) Paper Texture (m) © rawpixel.com; **3** *cla*: (ic) Play (m) © Adrien Coquet, thenounproject.com, CC BY-SA 3.0; **6,8,10,12,14** *tl* & **7,9,11,13,15** *tr*: (ic) Newspaper (m) © Loic Poivet, thenounproject.com, CC BY-SA 3.0; **6-15** *c*: (ph) Book (m) © Robert Armstrong, pixabay.com; **16,18,20,22** *tl* & **17,19,21,23** *tr*: (ic) Birthday Calendar (m) © Kiran Shastry, thenounproject.com, CC BY-SA 3.0; **16-25, 42-61, 84-92** *w*: (m)(ph) Concrete Terrazzo Wall (m) © rawpixel.com; **16** *cla* & **19** *clb*: (ic) Television (m) © Adrien Coquet, thenounproject.com, CC BY-SA 3.0; **16** *clb*: (ic) Book (m) © Travis Avery, thenounproject.com, CC BY-SA 3.0; **17** *cla*: (ic) Cricket (m) © SANB, thenounproject.com, CC BY-SA 3.0; **23,24** *cla* & **17** *clb*: (ic) Theatre (m) © Ben Davis, thenounproject.com, CC BY-SA 3.0; **18** *cla*: (ic) Sculpture (m) © Creative Mania, thenounproject.com, CC BY-SA 3.0; **21** *cla* & **18,24** *clb*: (ic) Clapper Board (m) © Andrew Nielsen, thenounproject.com, CC BY-SA 3.0; **19** *cla*: (ic) Football (m) © leo-graph.com, thenounproject.com, CC BY-SA 3.0; **20,22** *cla* & **21,22** *clb*: (ic) Microphone (m) © andriwidodo, thenounproject.com, CC BY-SA 3.0; **20** *clb*: (ic) Speaker (m) © popcornarts, thenounproject.com, CC BY-SA 3.0; **23** *clb*: (ic) Baby (m) © Emily Keller, thenounproject.com, CC BY-SA 3.0; **24** *tl* & **25** *tr*: (ic) Wreath (m) © Alex Muravev, thenounproject.com, CC BY-SA 3.0; **24** *cl*: (ic) Noose (m) © Manos Hatzidakis, thenounproject.com, CC BY-SA 3.0; **25** *cla* & **25** *cl*: (ic) Palette (m) © ciciliakwo, thenounproject.com, CC BY-SA 3.0; **25** *clb*: (ic) physics (m) © Tru3_Art, thenounproject.com, CC BY-SA 3.0; **26-40** *w*: (m)(ph) White Concrete Wall (m) © rawpixel.com; **26** *tl* & **27** *tr*: (ic) Coins (m) © Evgenii Likhachov, thenounproject.com, CC BY-SA 3.0; **28** *tl*: (ic) Army (m) © Viral faisalovers, thenounproject.com, CC BY-SA 3.0; **29** *tr*: (ic) Office (m) © Anggara Putra, thenounproject.com, CC BY-SA 3.0; **30** *tl*: (ic) Tractor (m) © Olivier Guin, thenounproject.com, CC BY-SA 3.0; **31** *tr*: (ic) School Desk (m) © Jongrak, thenounproject.com, CC BY-SA 3.0; **32** *tl*: (ic) Exams (m) © Arjan Farzkenari, thenounproject.com, CC BY-SA 3.0; **33** *tr*: (ic) Children (m) © IronSV, thenounproject.com, CC BY-SA 3.0; **34** *tl* & **35** *tr*: (ic) Home (m) © Numero Uno, thenounproject.com, CC BY-SA 3.0; **36** *tl*: (ic) roast chicken (m) © Slurp Design (m) © faisalovers, thenounproject.com, CC BY-SA 3.0; **37** *tr*: (ic) Fruit (m) © novani thenounproject.com, CC BY-SA 3.0; **38** *tl* & **39** *tr*: (ic) Fashion (m) © Mahmure Alp, thenounproject.com, CC BY-SA 3.0; **40** *tl*: (ic) Holiday (m) © Claudia Revalina, thenounproject.com, CC BY-SA 3.0; **41** *tr*: (ic) Christmas Tree (m) © Azam Ishaq, thenounproject.com, CC BY-SA 3.0; **41** *w*: Christmas (m) © Annie Spratt, unsplash.com; **42** *tr*: (ic) Entertainment (m) © shashank singh, thenounproject.com, CC BY-SA 3.0; **43,45** *tr* & **44** *tl*: (ic) Clapper Board (m) © Andrew Nielsen, thenounproject.com, CC BY-SA 3.0; **46** *tl* & **47** *tr*: (ic) Radio (m) © GreenHill, thenounproject.com, CC BY-SA 3.0; **48** *tl* & **49** *tr*: (ic) Television (m) © Adrien Coquet, thenounproject.com, CC BY-SA 3.0; **50,52** *tl* & **51** *tr*: (ic) Record (m) © Mourad Mokrane, thenounproject.com, CC BY-SA 3.0; **53** *tr*: (ic) Music Note (m) © karen tyler, thenounproject.com, CC BY-SA 3.0; **54** *tl* & **55** *tr*: (ic) Trumpet (m) © Valter Bispo, thenounproject.com, CC BY-SA 3.0; **56** *tl*: (ic) Arts (m) © Kelsey Armstrong, thenounproject.com, CC BY-SA 3.0; **57,59** *tr* & **58** *tl*: (ic) Book (m) © Travis Avery, thenounproject.com, CC BY-SA 3.0; **60** *tl*: (ic) Sculpture (m) © Creative Mania, thenounproject.com, CC BY-SA 3.0; **61** *tr*: (ic) Poetry (m) © Martin, thenounproject.com, CC BY-SA 3.0; **62** *tl*: (ic) Old Computer (m) © Juicy Fishs, thenounproject.com, CC BY-SA 3.0; **63** *tr*: (ic) Washing Machine (m) © Nun, thenounproject.com, CC BY-SA 3.0; **64** *tl* & **65** *tr*: (ic) Nuclear (m) © Adrien Coquet, thenounproject.com, CC BY-SA 3.0; **66** *tl*: (ic) Test Tube (m) © b farias, thenounproject.com, CC BY-SA 3.0; **67** *tr*: (ic) nobel peace prize (m) © Tom Fricker, thenounproject.com, CC BY-SA 3.0; **68** *tl*: (ic) Code (m) © Gregor Cresnar, thenounproject.com, CC BY-SA 3.0; **68** *w*: (ph) Turing Machine (m) © Wikimedia Commons, CC BY-SA 3.0; **69** *tr*: (ic) Elvis (m) © Ariel Kotzer, thenounproject.com, CC BY-SA 3.0; **69** *w*: (ph) Microphone (m) © Leo Weiling, unsplash.com; **70** *tl*: (ic) Mountain (m) © rasendria, thenounproject.com, CC BY-SA 3.0; **70** *w*: (ph) K2 (m) © Zacharie Grossen, Wikimedia Commons, CC BY-SA 3.0; **71** *tr*: (ic) Avalanche (m) © Lima Studio, thenounproject.com, CC BY-SA 3.0; **71** *w*: (ph) Snow (m) © Will Turner, unsplash.com; **72** *tl*: (ic) Vampire (m) © Grégory Montigny, thenounproject.com, CC BY-SA 3.0; **72** *w*: (ph) Graveyard (m) © Matthias Müllner, unsplash.com; **73** *tr*: (ic) Meteorite (m) © Valeriy, thenounproject.com, CC BY-SA 3.0; **73** *w*: (ph) Earth (m) © Javier Miranda, unsplash.com; **74** *tl*: (ic) boeing b 29 superfortress (m) © usubaliev, thenounproject.com, CC BY-SA 3.0; **74** *w*: (ph) Lancaster Bomber (m) © Paul, adobestock.com; **75** *tr*: (ic) Life Ring (m) © Made, thenounproject.com, CC BY-SA 3.0; **75** *w*: (ph) Sea (m) © Giga Khurtsilava, unsplash.com; **76** *tl*: (ic) Football (m) © leo-graph.com, thenounproject.com, CC BY-SA 3.0; **76** *w*: Football Pitch (m) © Alberto Frías, unsplash.com; **77** *tr*: (ic) Tennis (m) © Mister Pixel, thenounproject.com, CC BY-SA 3.0; **77** *w*: Tennis Court (m) © Max Zindel, unsplash.com; **78** *tl*: (ic) Rugby Ball (m) © Marco Livolsi, thenounproject.com, CC BY-SA 3.0; **78** *w*: Rugby Match (m) © Alex Motoc, unsplash.com; **78** *h*: Rugby Lineout © Auckland Museum, Wikimedia Commons, CC BY-SA 3.0; **79** *tr*: (ic) Cricket (m) © Bernd Lakenbrink, thenounproject.com, CC BY-SA 3.0; **79** *w*: Cricketer (m) © Yogendra Singh, unsplash.com; **80** *tl*: (ic) Horse Racing (m) © Sergio Morozov, thenounproject.com, CC BY-SA 3.0; **80** *w*: Racehorse (m) © Luisa Peter, unsplash.com; **80** *h*: Horse Race © Jongsun Lee, Wikimedia Commons, CC BY-SA 3.0; **81** *tr*: (ic) Relay (m) © Adrien Coquet, thenounproject.com, CC BY-SA 3.0; **81** *w*: (ph) Athletics Track (m) © Markus Spiske, unsplash.com; **82** *tl*: (ic) Boxing Glove (m) © Anton Anuchin, thenounproject.com, CC BY-SA 3.0; **82** *w*: Boxing Match (m) © Johann Walter Bantz, unsplash.com; **83** *tr*: (ic) Golfer (m) © Nicolas Vicent, thenounproject.com, CC BY-SA 3.0; **83** *w*: Golfing (m) © Courtney Cook, unsplash.com; **83** *h*: Golf Ball (m) © mk. s, unsplash.com; **84,86,88** *tl* & **85,87,89** *tr*: (ic) Framed Picture (m) © Lil Squid, thenounproject.com, CC BY-SA 3.0; **90** *tl* & **91** *tr*: (ic) Camera (m) © AomAm, thenounproject.com, CC BY-SA 3.0; **92** *tl*: (ic) Present (m) © Vinzence Studio, thenounproject.com, CC BY-SA 3.0

1954 : What A Year To Be Born!
Why not join our mailing list...

Answers to the Eleven-plus Exam on page 32

Arithmetic Questions

Q1: The motorist has travelled 202 miles

Q2: 314

Q3: The ship could travel 120 miles

Q4: Four hundred and sixty five

Q5: A) Elizabeth's father was 36 years old

Q5: B) In 7 years' time

Q5: C) Elizabeth will be 30 years old

General Intelligence Questions

Q1: A) **Billy** was stung by **a** bee.

Q1: B) The shepherd **stood** by the gate and **whistled** to his dog.

Q1: C) The **family** went to the pool for a **swim**.

Q2: A) Coconut

Q2: B) Giraffe

Q2: C) Patricia

Q3: A) When the dog saw me, it wagged **its** tail.

Q3: B) The subject doesn't concern you or **me**.

Q3: C) Whilst speaking to my brother, the police car **passed** me.

Printed in Great Britain
by Amazon

47677183R00053